YOU CAN'T HANDLE THE TRUTH!

YOU CAN'T HANDLE THE TRUTH!

What's Really Happening in America

CRAIG NEDROW

XULON PRESS

Xulon Press
555 Winderley Pl, Suite 225
Maitland, FL 32751
407.339.4217
www.xulonpress.com

Xulon
PRESS

Paperback ISBN-13: 978-1-66288-661-4
Ebook ISBN-13: 978-1-66288-662-1

First and foremost, I want to thank the Lord for leading me in writing my second book. His grace and mercy He continues to show me overwhelms me with gratitude.

I also want to give a special thank you to my wife, best friend and partner in life Micah. You encouraged me to write both books and without you I wouldn't have achieved either of them. You truly are my better half and I thank God for you daily.

Thanks to Brad & Aleisha for allowing me to be their father and to all four of my grandchildren who help to keep me young.

I would also like to thank the many pastors, friends, associates and family members for your love, support and encouragement over the years since Jesus changed my life and took me in a totally different direction. Your support is more valuable to me than you will ever know.

My prayer is that this book will open dialogue and create a clear reflection on where we are at as a nation without political agendas.

I love my country and I consider myself a patriot and want the very best for America!

May the Lord bless all who read this book!

—Craig Nedrow

Introduction

—m—

How did we, as a nation, get to this place? How does a nation slide so far down so fast? Is it already too late to turn this thing around? Do the majority of Americans really even care anymore? What will this nation look like in another forty years, or twenty, or even ten? Do people honestly want to know the truth about what has happened to our nation?

These are all questions that we will attempt to address in this book.

In the movie *A Few Good Men*, there is a classic scene toward the end of the film with Jack Nicholson and Tom Cruise. This scene takes place in the courtroom when Nicholson is on the witness stand and Cruise is hammering him for answers. At the peak of this scene, Nicholson says to Cruise, "What do you want from me?" And Cruise says, "I want the truth." Nicholson responds very strongly to him, "You can't handle the truth!"[1] That response is the inspiration for the title of this book.

---

[1] Reiner, Brown, Scheinman, "A Few Good Men", 1992

I strongly believe that we, as a nation, have been deceived. And I also believe that many people either don't want to know the truth or can't handle the truth. In my opinion, we have been deceived into believing that the bible isn't God's word. We have been deceived into believing that we have progressed as a society and that the things God calls wrong are somehow ok now and that His word is no longer relevant. I believe we have switched our attention to things that are taking us down a very dark path and I am concerned that we may not be able to find our way back.

I will attempt to peel back layer by layer and expose the deception that has taken the greatest nation in the history of mankind to the point that we're at now. When an onion is peeled layer by layer, tears inevitably follow. And as I have watched, prayed, and sought the Lord through prayer and His word concerning America today, there have been tears.

I will be candid and to the point. You may not agree with some, part, or all of what I write. That's okay. I'm not trying to write a "feel good" book here. What I am attempting is to sound the warning trumpet as the Lord is leading me to do.

I will base what is said in this book on Scripture, the word of God. There are two reasons for that. First, the word of God is the truth. Whether you or I believe that or not has no bearing on the fact that His word is the truth. I'm not God, and neither are you. Only God is God, and His Word is true, no matter what we may think. Secondly, Scripture is the one constant. Everything we see and touch will be gone one day, but God's word will remain. Jesus said, "Heaven and earth will pass away, but My words will by no means pass away" (Matt. 24:35 NKJV).

Please notice that Jesus said, "by no means." Nothing will cause His words to pass away. The Bible was relevant when it was written; it's just as relevant in our world today, and it will always be relevant.

Are the economic problems we face a threat to America? Yes.
Is terrorism a threat to America? Yes.
Is our national debt a threat to America? Yes.

All these are threats to America, but they're really just the manifestation of a more deeply rooted problem. I can cut weeds in my yard, but they will come back over and over until I get to the root. So, let's dig deep. Let's get to the root of the problem. Let's examine, from the truth of Scripture, what God says is wrong with us.

I sincerely believe the day may come when my grandchildren will ask, and rightfully so, "Poppy, why did you guys let this happen?" What will we answer to future generations about why we allowed this to happen to America? I love my country, but I don't recognize the America that I grew up in just a few short years ago. We must take a very serious, difficult look at what is happening. And we must do it right now before it's too late!

Here is a quote that I think is worthy of meditation.

The average age of the world's greatest civilizations has been 200 years. These nations have progressed through this sequence:

From bondage to spiritual faith;
From spiritual faith to great courage;
From courage to liberty;
From liberty to abundance;
From abundance to selfishness;
From selfishness to apathy;
From apathy to dependence;
From dependence back into bondage.[2]

Please stop, think about this quote, and ask yourself this question: Where is America in this sequence?

---

[2] Commonly attributed to Alexander Fraser Tytler

Table of Contents

—𝔪—

Chapter 1

What Is Truth?

—∞—

Webster defines *truth* as: "the real facts about something."[3]
In Psalm 51:6 NKJV, David says of God: "Behold, You desire truth in the inward parts." God wants the truth because He is the truth.

In John 18, Jesus spoke with Pontus Pilate, and said: "Pilate therefore said to Him, "Are You a king then?" Jesus answered, "You say rightly that I am a king. For this cause I was born, and for this cause I have come into the world, that I should bear witness to the truth. Everyone who is of the truth hears My voice" (John 18:37 NKJV).

I will make a bold statement here regarding Jesus's words, "Everyone who is of the truth hears my voice." To a large degree in America today, **we are losing the desire and/or ability to hear the truth of God's word.**

If you examine what is taking place from a spiritual standpoint in America today, I believe you will observe

---

[3] Merriam-Webster, inc. 2023

that the large majority of the population spends little or no serious time studying God's word. I'm not talking about attending church or even being in a weekly Bible study. Those are wonderful things. What I mean by "serious time" is this: being still, becoming quiet by yourself and then pray.

Ask the Holy Spirit to lead and show you what you need to see and hear from God's word. Don't be in a hurry to try and read a certain number of verses or chapters. Let the Holy Spirit lead you. Take the time to really think about and meditate on the word. Psalm 46:10 says, **"Be still and know that I am God."** Open the Scriptures and spend time with the Father. When you do this, He will reveal life-changing things to you.

Knowing that the word of God is true, if we don't spend serious time in it, we open ourselves up to become easily deceived by the enemy and the world. How can I really know if something is a lie if I don't know what the truth is? Spending this time in the word gives us discernment and a sensitivity to distinguish right from wrong, dark from light, and good from evil. When a nation of people doesn't have that discernment, it will be easier to deceive them.

God says in Jeremiah 33:3 NKJV, "Call to Me, and I will answer you, and show you great and mighty things, which you do not know." I love this verse!

Also in John 17 NKJV; Jesus prayed to God the Father, and in verse 17, He said: "Sanctity them by Your truth. Your word is truth."

The devil has done an amazing job of deceiving people into thinking that the word of God is no longer relevant or that it's really not the word of God at all. I hear people say, "The Bible was written by men, not God." Here's my answer to that: That is a lie from the enemy of your soul. "Knowing this first, that no prophecy of Scripture is of any private interpretation, for prophecy never came by the will of man, but holy men of God spoke as they were moved by the Holy Spirit" (2 Pet. 1:20–21 NKJV) And: "All Scripture is given by inspiration of God, and is profitable for doctrine, for reproof, for correction, for instruction in righteousness" (2 Tim. 3:16 NKJV). The word *inspiration* means "God breathed" in the original Greek.[4]

I find it astounding that people will read something on the internet or hear something on the news and just assume that it's the truth, but they will question the Bible.

As someone who has studied the Bible exhaustively for the better part of twenty years, without any hesitation, I can absolutely tell you that the Bible is the word of God and that it is all true. In Proverbs, it says: "Every word of God is pure; He is a shield to those who put their trust in Him" (Prov. 30:5 NKJV).

It grieves me when I witness the treatment of the word of God. I know people who have said to me: "Do you really believe the Bible is the word of God?" And I will say, "Yes, I do," and they will almost snicker at me like I am naïve. But of all those people who have asked me that, I always ask them this simple question: "Have you ever studied, and I mean really studied, the

---

4 Merriam-Webster, inc. 2023

Bible from cover to cover?" And not a single one has ever said, "Yes, and I can tell you that the Bible is not the word of God." You see, I don't believe a person can sincerely study this book with an open mind and come to that conclusion. Here's what will happen. The Holy Spirit will reveal Himself, and that person will come to know the truth.

That's exactly what happened to a man named Josh McDowell. He wrote a book titled *Evidence That Demands a Verdict*. In this book, Mr. McDowell started out to disprove Christianity and the Bible, and what happened instead is that he became one of the great apologists of our time.[5]

If you are a sincere skeptic and really want to do some research, then I would recommend you get his book and read it. By the way, I have never met Josh McDowell. My point is that I have no motive for you to read his book other than to encourage you to do the research and then make your conclusion.

The greatest way to know whether the Bible truly is God's word is to spend quality time alone, with a humble, open mind in His word, and then make your decision. Also, please notice the verse in Proverbs 30, where we are told that God "is a shield to those who put their trust in Him."

For so long in America, we believed the Bible and trusted in God, and He shielded us from things we don't even fully know about. But when a nation begins

---

[5] McDowell, *Evidence That Demands a Verdict*

to rebel against God, He will eventually begin to remove His hand of protection.

I've titled this book: "You Can't Handle the Truth." Well, here is probably the greatest truth that most people can't handle: **As a nation of people, to a large degree, we have turned away from God and His word.**

Allow me to support that statement. All through the Bible, one of the consistent themes is this: God says over and over again to His people, "If you will trust Me, and obey Me, things will go well for you. I will protect you, and take care of you. I will provide for you, and bless you. I will defeat your enemies, and direct your steps. You will prosper in all areas of life, and you will have peace" (Deut. 28 NKJV). Any serious student of the Bible will confirm that this is a consistent message from God to His people.

When Israel trusted in God, things went well. And when they turned from God, they suffered. So, let me ask: When was the last time America was at peace? When was the last time we were at rest? Why do we now have problems that we don't have answers for? Why do we have violence in our streets, corruption at every level of our society, disrespect for authority, and the loss of morals and values that made us such a great nation?

I will give several difficult truths in this book, but they will all funnel back to this one simple truth: **We have turned from God and His word!**

Let me ask you a question: As a nation of people, if we absolutely knew that turning back to God and submitting to His Word would heal our land and fix our problems, why wouldn't we simply **do** that? We will examine that question in the chapters to follow.

Chapter 2
The Role of a Watchman

—⚏—

I remember the first time I came across the following verses:

> "Son of man, I have made you a watchman for the house of Israel; therefore hear a word from My mouth, and give them warning from Me: When I say to the wicked, "You shall surely die," and you give him no warning, nor speak to warn the wicked from his wicked way, to save his life, that same wicked man shall die in his iniquity; but his blood I will require at your hand. Yet, if you warn the wicked, and he does not turn from his wicked way, he shall die in his iniquity; but you have delivered your soul" (Ezek. 3:17–19 NKJV).

The role of a "watchman" is not a popular one. Our human nature is that we don't want correction. Pride and rebellion rise up within us as we think, "Who are you to criticize me?" So let me address here why I feel the need to speak out in a "watchman" role.

The Bible speaks about the "body of Christ" and refers to the fact that there are many parts of the body, and they don't all have the same function. In the human body, the ears obviously function in a different capacity than the eyes and so on. The same is true in a spiritual manner. Here is a good example: Greg Laurie functions as an evangelist in the body of Christ. John Hagee functions in a completely different capacity. Some would call him a "fire and brimstone" preacher. Both are effective and necessary in the body of Christ.

The first time I came across these verses in Ezekiel, I knew the watchman calling would be part of my ministry. It's not an easy message to deliver, but God sends warnings, and some of us are called to deliver those warnings.

I believe that one of the reasons for this calling over my life is because the Lord did such a deep correction in me. If you've read my first book *Free Indeed*, then you know how the Lord took me, broke me behind the walls of a prison, and transformed my life. God then calls many of the people He breaks like that to be a witness and warn others.

In the book of Acts: the apostle Paul, who God first blinded, then called on the road to Damascus to be a powerful witness, said, "I testify to you this day that I am innocent of the blood of all men. For I have not shunned to declare to you the whole counsel of God" (Acts 20:26–27 NKJV).

Paul was a witness for Christ, but he also spoke out boldly against the darkness. He said:

"Let no one deceive you with empty words, for because of these things the wrath of God comes upon the sons of disobedience. Therefore do not be partakers with them. For you were once darkness, but now you are light in the Lord. Walk as children of light (for the fruit of the Spirit is in all goodness, righteousness, and truth), finding out what is acceptable to the Lord. And have no fellowship with the unfruitful works of darkness, but rather expose them" (Eph. 5:6–11 NKJV).

And expose them, he did! Paul was a warrior for Christ, and he didn't candy-coat the message. Paul's ministry was a difficult one. All watchman ministries are difficult. Two of the greatest watchmen ever were Jeremiah and Isaiah. Jeremiah was thrown into prison, as was Paul, and both had their lives threatened on several occasions. Tradition tells us that Isaiah was sawn in two.[6] That absolutely amazes me. "The Prophet," Isaiah, sawn in two. WOW!

In the time of the Old Testament, most of the towns had a wall around the perimeter. The role of a watchman was to sit on the wall, peer into the distance, and watch for any approaching enemy. When he saw the enemy, he would blow a trumpet to warn the people. That's where we get the term "warning trumpet."

Now apply that to the spiritual realm. When the enemy, Satan, is on the attack, a watchman's role is to blow the warning trumpet to warn the people.

---

[6] Hebrews 11:37 NKJV

"But Craig, wouldn't it just be *so* much easier to just preach on all the promises blessings of God and just make people feel better about themselves?" Of course, it would, but that's not what God called these watchmen of the past to do, and that's not what He calls some of us to do today.

If there was ever a time for watchman voices to emerge on the scene in America, that time is **now**!

The question is not just "Where are the watchmen?" but also "Will the people listen to the warning?" In my opinion, we've lost the "watchman" voices in America, **and** most people are not listening, nor do they care to listen.

We have grown **so** comfortable and complacent in America that we either don't want to be bothered with the warnings, or we just want to bury our heads in the sand and live as though there is nothing wrong. But most of us know deep down that something is tragically wrong with our country right now.

Let me ask you this: How can a just God destroy Sodom and Gomorrah for their sexual immorality but then **not** hold us accountable for the sexual immorality of America? There is such a spirit of deception that has engulfed our nation today. To hear the leaders of our nation say, "We've evolved as a society," and what was once considered an abomination is now celebrated is a testament to how far and fast we are sliding into demise.

I am just one man seeking the Lord and to the best of my ability, trying to be obedient to what He puts in front of me. I know that there is a watchman calling in my ministry, and I am writing this book to help sound the trumpet. So let me say this as clearly as I know how: **We have turned from God and His word**.

The devil is destroying our nation from within. We are morally and spiritually rotting from the inside. And unless we, as a nation of people, confess our sin of rebellion against God, repent, and return to Him, we will be destroyed.

This is not easy to hear or admit, is it? Remember, the role of a watchman is not easy, nor is it popular.

I hear people say: "Our best years are still ahead of us, Craig." Really? And you base that on what exactly?

Folks, the signs are everywhere! Here are just a few:

- The national debt: $30+ trillion
- Corruption at unprecedented levels
- Violence throughout our land so out of control that there are entire communities where the police won't even go into any more.
- Lawlessness has exploded in America.
- Celebrating what God calls evil; and what God says is good, we now call hate speech.
- A country that is divided more than any time in the last one hundred years.
- The loss of patriotism
- The influx of foreigners who do not share or care to share our values.
- The silencing of the church
- Disobedience to parents and authority
- The moral decline of our nation

- The liberal indoctrination of our children in our schools

In Isaiah, the Bible says: "Woe to those who call evil good, and good evil; Who put darkness for light, and light for darkness; Who put bitter for sweet, and sweet for bitter!" (Isa. 5:20 NKJV). The word "Woe" is an old Hebrew word that was used in a courtroom setting and meant "Guilty as charged, and sentencing impending.[7]

God pronounces a woe on those who "call evil good and good evil, who put darkness for light and light for darkness." We are there, people, and I repeat, the signs are everywhere! **Please, folks, hear the warning of the trumpets!**

---

[7] Strong's Concordance

Chapter 3

Political Correctness:
The Road to Hell!

—⚉—

A sk yourself this question, who coined the phrase *political correctness*, and how did it become such a high priority in our country? I challenge you that this thing we call political correctness is leading us as a nation down the road to hell. Allow me to expand a bit on this thought.

It started with a small group of people who had some very radical ideas about many of our nation's morals, values, and the direction that this nation should be headed. These people slowly began to profess ideas and values that, until recently, simply would not have been accepted nor tolerated in America.

Their method of operation is simple. Speak out about ideas often enough and loud enough and be relentless in doing so, and people will eventually go along with these ideas. They have proven that if they talk louder, interrupt any opposition to their ideas, name-call, label, and remain persistent about their agenda, they can mold and turn the masses in their direction. This is a form of brainwashing, and they have been hugely successful.

Think about it. Things that we **know** are wrong have become tolerated and celebrated in our nation today because of the political correctness that is destroying our country. We are more concerned about offending someone than speaking the truth.

Stop and reflect on some of the areas that political correctness now affect:

- We are no longer to believe and speak out about the fact that marriage is supposed to be between one man and one woman.
- We have to be very careful about what Scriptures we can quote, teach, preach, and even believe in.
- New translations of the Bible are scrubbing all mention of sin and hell because some people are offended by that.
- Prayer in public is now being outlawed in many places because it may offend someone. (Do you find it odd that it's okay to stand around in a small group and tell filthy stories, but God forbid we should get quiet, bow our heads, and pray? **Really**?)
- We must be careful about what we say about Muslims, Islam, and terrorists, but it's open season on Christianity.
- We now must be sensitive to calling someone a "boy" or "girl" because it may offend them.
- We are at the point where people who have been born male and female can decide to change their

sex, and we're not to think that's odd, much less actually express that we think it's odd.

- We are now supposed to believe that it's somehow okay to kill babies in the womb until birth, and in some places, even after birth.

We are reaching a point of **insanity** with all this political correctness, and where does it end? At some point, we must say, "Enough is enough!"

There is a verse that has captured me lately. We should all heed these words: Psalm 9:17 NKJV says, "The wicked shall be turned into hell. And all the nations that forget God."

As we continue down this road of political correctness, we are being drawn further and further away from God and His word.

Is this **NOT** evident to all of us? And why are we allowing this to happen in America today?

I grew up in an America where people trusted and respected the word of God. As a student of the Bible, it just makes sense. The spiritual backbone in our country is gone because the church has been silenced through complacency and political correctness.

It is my opinion that we are a nation that has grown fat, and we are a spoiled, lazy, self-centered society. There are those who are set on destroying the fabric of our nation, and they are succeeding. I am only one man, but I truly love my nation, and I must speak up and do what I can before it's too late.

I would like to share another section of Scripture about what is happening in America today. The LORD is speaking here:

"I brought you into a bountiful country,
To eat its fruit and its goodness.
But when you entered, you defiled My land.
And made My heritage an abomination.
The priests did not say, 'Where is the LORD?'
And those who handle the law did not know Me;
The rulers also transgressed against Me;
The prophets prophesied by Baal,
And walked after things that do not profit.
"Therefore I will yet bring charges against you,"
  says the LORD,
"And against your children's children I will bring charges."

"Has a nation changed its gods,
Which are not gods?
But My people have changed their Glory
For what does not profit.
Be astonished, O heavens, at this,
And be horribly afraid;
Be very desolate," says the LORD,
"For My people have committed two evils;
They have forsaken Me, the fountain of living waters,
And hewn (dug) for themselves cisterns—
broken cisterns that can hold no water."

Have you not brought this on yourself,
In that you have forsaken the LORD your God

When He led you in the way?

"Your own wickedness will correct you
And your backslidings will rebuke you
Know therefore and see that it is
an evil and bitter thing
That you have forsaken the LORD
your God
And the fear of Me is not in you,"
Says the Lord God of hosts" (Jer. 2:7–9,11–13, 17, 19 NKJV).

My, oh my, what an amazing and sobering set of verses from Jeremiah. Allow me to make a few points about these verses:

First, it's **God** who brought us into and gave us a great nation! It's the height of arrogance for us as a people to think that the blessings that have been given to us are **not** from God.

Second, as Jeremiah addressed five groups of people, it is my opinion that this applies to our nation today as well.

1) The priests did not say, "Where is the LORD?" Priests here represent the spiritual leaders of the nation.
2) "And those who handle the law did not know Me." These represent those in Washington who make laws for the nation. Think about this; if those that make laws knew the Lord, they wouldn't put laws on the books that go contrary to the His word. They've obviously lost the fear of the Lord.

3) "The rulers also transgressed against Me." The rulers are the people in power, whether it be money, influence, or the direction of a nation.

4) "The prophets prophesied by Baal, and walked after things that do not profit." These represent those who speak about the things to come for a nation. Instead of keeping God and His word in pre-eminence, they were led astray, which in turn led the people down roads of destruction.

5) "But My people have changed their Glory." This represents the masses. We have been seduced, deceived, and led astray from God and the things of God to the point where we are now.

Third, as verse 17 above states, have we have not brought this on ourselves, in that we have forgotten the LORD our God when He led us in the way?

The problems we are facing in this country today that we don't have the answers for are our own fault because the political correctness of a few have led us astray when we should have stood up and said, **"Not on our watch!"**

Fourth, "Your own wickedness will correct you." We don't enjoy hearing about the correction of the LORD. But the Bible says, "Do not despise the chastening of the LORD, nor detest His correction; for whom the LORD loves He corrects" (Prov. 3:11–12 NKJV). But please don't miss that the correction is because of our own wickedness as a nation.

Finally, "You have forsaken the LORD your God; and the fear of Me is not in you." Many will say, "Craig, that's Old Testament stuff." Okay, well listen to what Jesus said in the New Testament, "Do not fear those who kill the body but cannot kill the soul. But rather fear Him who is able to destroy both soul and body in hell" (Matt. 10:28 NKJV). Does that make you uncomfortable? It should!

Many years ago, an older man I knew told me that we, as nation, were in real trouble. When I asked him to expand, he said, "We've lost the fear of the Lord in this nation, and because of that, we are in real serious trouble." I couldn't agree more. The political correctness that is rampant in our nation today reflects a society that has lost reverence for the Lord, and this political correctness is worsening at an alarming rate. I believe that one day soon, I might not be allowed to write a book like this.

I repeat: **Political correctness is taking us down the road to hell.**

Chapter 4

We've Lost Our Minds!

—∿—

I have a radio program called *Stand Up 4 Jesus*, which has been on the air throughout Texas and Oklahoma since 2010. Several times over the last few years, I have found myself saying, "Ladies and gentlemen, we, as a nation of people, have officially **lost our minds**!" And the sad fact is that I'm not kidding. I know **many** of you agree with me as you watch today's current events that we are spiraling out of control. The absolute insanity that we are witnessing is what tells me we are in real trouble.

Yes, as you probably can guess, I am a conservative. But here is what I mean by *conservatism*. I believe in Jesus Christ as the Son of God. I believe that He came, born of a virgin, lived a sinless life, died on the cross for my sins and your sins, rose on the third day, then ascended to heaven, sits on the right hand of God the Father, and that one day soon, He will come again. I also believe that the Bible is the written word of God, from the opening chapter of Genesis to the closing chapter of Revelation. I believe it was relevant when it was written and that it's still relevant today. I believe that we, as a nation, have been deceived and that we have grown lukewarm concerning the things of God, and that we are being destroyed morally and spiritually from within. I believe in respect for your elders (now there's a phrase you don't hear very often anymore, which we will discuss later), that my "yes should mean yes," and my "no should mean no," that I should stand up and speak up for the things I value, that I love my country and believe that anyone who doesn't want to be here should simply find somewhere else to go, that Americans should stand up for Americans, and that we **must** repent as a nation before it's too late. This is my definition of a conservative. It may not be yours, but I believe that you should be able to express your opinion, and so should I.

Now back to why I believe that as a nation, **"we've lost our minds**."

By this time, knowing me as you do, it should come as no surprise that I want to share Scripture with you. In Romans 12, Apostle Paul writes: "Do not be conformed to this world, but be transformed by the renewing of your mind" (Rom. 12:2 NKJV). Paul tells us clearly **not** to be conformed to this world. What does that mean? Well, the word *conformed* in the Greek language is the word "Suschematizo," where we get our English word *Schematic,* and here it means "to fashion oneself according to," or "to conform to the same pattern.[8] Paul warns us here **not** to be conformed to the world.

---

[8] Strong's Concordance

What does that mean in the context of what I am talking about? It means that just because everybody else is going along with something doesn't make it right. Just because the "world" or society says something is right doesn't make it right. Reflect back on times in your life when you've heard or read something and thought, "That just doesn't sound right." I really believe we as a nation of people are losing that sensitivity to distinguish between right and wrong.

The second part of that verse in Romans is "be transformed by the renewing of your mind." How do we renew our minds? First, let me tell you how you **don't** renew your mind. What we take in through the radio, television, movies, internet, and from other people is so important. We are bombarded by **so** much junk today that a person must be intentional about guarding their minds. Things that in the past would appall us we now laugh at and are numb to. I said this before, but it bears repeating: we as a nation are morally and spiritually rotting from the inside out because we are conforming to the world and not renewing our minds.

So, how do we renew our minds? There are three things needed for the renewal of the mind:

1. Getting still with God.
2. Prayer
3. Go back to God's word.

1. "Be still and know that I am God" (Ps. 46:10 NKJV). We must re-learn the practice of getting still. We are

so busy today (which is a tool of the devil) that most of us simply can't imagine finding time to get still. What do I mean by "to get still"? Turn your phone **off**, get away from people somewhere, ask the Holy Spirit to help you to clear your mind of all the junk that's surrounding you, and begin to meditate on God and who He really is. Realize that He is still on the throne and knows everything going on in your life. Realize that He is God during the good and hard times. He is the God who can change circumstances, open doors that no man can open, close doors that no man can close, His plans are good, not evil, and He cares for you more than you are able to comprehend.

Getting still allows us to get our minds de-cluttered from the things that bring chaos into our lives. It helps us to get our focus off of ourselves and onto God. One of the main reasons we can't hear from God is because of all the clamor in our world today. Psalm 46:10 is one of my life verses. I **must** have my time to get still and be alone with God.

Jesus is always our greatest example, and this applies here. In Mark 1:35 NKJV, the Bible says, "Now in the morning, having risen a long while before daylight, He went out and departed to a solitary place; and there He prayed." If Jesus found it important to get still, do you think maybe we should learn from Him? Notice also that when He got still in a solitary place, "He prayed." That brings me to my next part of renewing the mind . . .

2. Prayer! In Philippians 4:7, the Bible tells us to pray about everything. When we get still, get our minds off ourselves, and turn our attention to God, it puts us into a place of fellowship with our heavenly Father. The Bible also tells us in Philippians to "let your requests be made known to God" (Philippians 4:7 NKJV) Do you think if you were to pray to God the Father and ask Him to help renew your mind that He would do that? It's really a dumb question if you think about it.

Imagine praying: "Lord, I ask You, in the name of Jesus, to renew my mind, that You would forgive me that I don't seek you more in this area. Father, I need my mind renewed. I want to think thoughts that are pleasing to You. I don't want to live in fear of the things going on around me in this world. I need Your peace. I need discernment to know between good and evil. I don't want worldly things to deceive me. I want to know the truth about things. I can't renew my mind on my own, so I am asking that Your Holy Spirit cleanse my mind, and that You would give me the peace I desperately need. Direct my thought life. Lord, I now give You my mind. Renew my mind as only You can in Jesus's name. Amen." Now . . . do you **not** think that God would honor that kind of prayer?

I have said this before on my radio program, and I want to state it here. If we really had a clear grasp on who it is we are praying to, it would radically change our prayer lives. Think about this; we have the privilege of praying to the Creator of the universe. He is able to change world circumstances in a moment. He tells us to "Cast all of your care upon Him, for He cares for you" (1 Pet. 5:7 NKJV). To me, that is an overwhelming thought.

When I wrote my first book, *Free Indeed*, I had a chapter on prayer, and when I began to write that chapter, I felt as though the Lord uttered to me, "Craig, your prayer life is an embarrassment to Me. If you had any idea who it is you're praying to, you would pray differently." I was shaken to my core, and I am reminded of that from time to time. I cannot over emphasize the importance that prayer plays in renewing our minds.

3. "Every word of God is pure" (Prov. 30:5 NKJV). We **must** get back to the word of God! In our world today, it has come to the point where people will say, "Just because something is true for you doesn't make it true for me." So, where can we go for the real truth? My answer to that should not surprise you. We go to the word of God. In Psalm 119:160 NKJV, the Bible says, "The entirety of Your word is truth." Please notice, "the entirety," which means all of it.

Let me take a bit of a detour here. Either something is true or not. I can't manipulate the truth, and neither can you. So, there must be a plum line that says, "This is true." For me, that plum line is the Bible.

If you happen to be one of those who say, "You don't really believe the Bible, do you?" Then you probably stopped reading this book quite some time ago. If someone doesn't believe the Bible is the word of God, then they certainly won't be receptive to all the Scripture in this book. I am attempting to look at things that are going wrong in our nation from a **biblical perspective**. If you don't agree, that's your choice.

I lived in rebellion from the Lord for forty years, then, by the grace of God, I was born again, and **everything** changed. My morals, values, viewpoints, decision-making, and choices in life took a radical turn. I became a student of God's word and began to study and research the Bible. I have spent the better part of the last twenty-five years studying this book, oftentimes for hours at a time.

Most people aren't aware of this, but over 3000 times in the Bible, it says, "Thus says the Lord," or "Hear the word of the Lord." Over 3000 times! Now, I'm not the smartest person walking around, and I don't know if it was the 83rd time or 756th time I read it, or when exactly, but at some point, the light went on in my mind that said, **"This must be the Word of the Lord!"** And if it **is** the word of the Lord, and it says that it's **all** true, then I made a conscious decision to trust and believe that it is what it says it is. It's really not that complicated, is it?

Now, back to renewing our minds. The word has a cleansing effect on our minds. Jesus said, "You are already clean because of the word which I have spoken to you" (John 15:3 NKJV). Here's what happens when we spend time in the word. The lies that we hear in the world every day get exposed. Instead of looking at things from our own viewpoint, we get God's perspective on those things. The factors that influence our way of thinking give way to the real truth, and a cleansing of the mind takes place.

Unfortunately, the devil has done a masterful job of gettin us all so busy that we don't take the time to get still and read, study, and meditate on God's word.

If we are to spend serious, quality time in the word, we must be intentional about it. It must become a priority that we do daily. We eat solid food because we need it for the nourishment of our bodies, but what about the nourishment of our spiritual bodies? The writer of Hebrews says it this way:

> "For though by this time you ought to be teachers, you need someone to teach you again the first principles of the oracles of God; and you have come to need milk and not solid food. For everyone who partakes only of milk is unskilled in the word of righteousness, for he is a babe. But solid food belongs to those who are of full age, that is, to those who by reason of use have their senses exercised to discern both good and evil" (Heb. 5:12–NKJV.)

When we spend serious time in the word, it "exercises our senses" and helps us to "discern between good and evil." You and I need to discern between good and evil in the world we live in today. The word helps us to do just that. We as a nation of people are malnourished in our spirits because most of us are starving from the lack of the word of God in our lives.

(4) "More than anything you guard, protect your mind, for life flows from it" (Prov. 4:23 CEB). The CEB Version of the Bible is the "Common English Bible,"

and I really like this version of Proverbs 4:23. The NKJV says, "Keep your heart with all diligence, for out of it spring the issues of life." This verse tells us that we must protect our minds and hearts from the garbage that is rampant in our society today. A person cannot expect to take garbage into their minds without it having a very serious negative effect on them. And yet, that is exactly what is happening.

I often wonder how I made it through life for so long without Jesus Christ. In the same aspect, I can't imagine not guarding my mind and heart against all the depravity that we face daily in our society today. Simply put, I can't watch, listen to, and read everything that's out there. There are movies that my wife Micah and I can't go see. There are parties that we don't get invited to, and that's okay. You may think that's goofy, and that's okay too.

Listen, if I want to protect my mind and my heart, then I have to be intentional about it. When I do guard my heart and mind, it honors my wife, honors the Lord, and keeps me from damaging my witness to the world around me.

So, let's go back to the title of this chapter: We've lost our minds.

The evidence is all around us. We are a nation that is clearly in moral decline. What we once knew was right, we now call wrong, and what we once called wrong, we now call right. Proverbs 14:6 NKJV says, "There is a way that seems right to a man, but it's end is the way of death." This verse can apply to a nation of people just as easily as to an individual. We are doing things in our country today that may seem right to some of the people, but without the leading of Christ in our nation, the result will be the death of America as we know it.

When a nation of people turns from the Lord, He removes His hand of blessing and protection, and the enemy attacks that nation in ways that will destroy that nation. That is happening here in America. This is why we have the number of problems now that we don't seem to have the answers for. As a result, we have lost our way and lost our minds in this country. We are more divided than we've ever been. We continue to kill the unborn and don't have the resolve to stop the killings. The church in America is more focused on buildings and watered-down messages than confronting the truth of what's really happening. The spiritual leaders have been intimidated into submission. I don't recognize the country I grew up in a few short years ago.

In the next chapter, we will look at how this has happened to the America that so many of us love and are very concerned about.

Chapter 5
It Didn't Happen Overnight

—꿍—

I hear people say, "How is this happening in America today?' That's the question I attempt to answer in this chapter.

As I write this book, I am now sixty-five years old. That in and of itself is a miracle of God. I would love to tell you that I was a pastor's kid and was always such a great kid, but that wouldn't be telling the truth. I was raised in a very good family from the aspect that my parents loved me, and I knew it, I have a brother and two sisters who I also knew loved me, and I grew up in a suburb of Dallas called Richardson, and it was a great place to grow up. But somewhere along the way, I began to make poor choices, and there are consequences for our choices in life. (I would like you to remember that last sentence as we will revisit it a bit later.) These choices took me down a dark path, and there were several years that I wasted running with the wrong crowd, doing the wrong things, and I eventually found myself in jail.

In Genesis 50, the Bible makes a reference that sometimes what the devil intends for evil, God intends for good. I don't wish this on anyone else, but for me, going to jail was the greatest thing that ever happened to me. This is where I became born again and discovered my life verse in Psalm 46:10 NKJV: "Be still and know that I am God." For me, it took going to jail to get still and realize that there is only **one true God**, and it wasn't me.

I tell you these things because sometimes it takes someone who has been on both sides of the fence to recognize the signs of a situation. Like the song "Amazing Grace" says: "I was lost, but now I'm found, I was blind, but now I see."

How does that apply to America and the place we find ourselves in today? Let's take a look at the last fifty years or so in America to find some answers. I will start out by quoting some phrases that used to mean something but seem to have lost their place today.

My dad used to tell me, "If a man's word is no good, then that man is no good." Today, it seems as though nobody cares if they have given their word on something. This may sound silly to some, but if I tell someone I am going to do something, I should do everything in my power to do what I said I would do.

Here's another: "Respect your elders." I mentioned that saying previously. If you're thirty or older, you've probably heard that phrase, and you know and understand exactly what it means. If you're under thirty, you probably think, "What a joke." But it's an important phrase and is a snapshot of what has happened in America. People older than yourself have tremendous wisdom that you can learn from. Even at my age now, when I have the chance to be around older people, I try to listen and learn something from their years of living.

It used to be that people would sit around in groups and tell stories and talk about what used to be important to this nation and the sacrifice that others have made for our nation. Most young people today have **no idea** the sacrifice previous generations have made for their freedom so they can live as they live. Past generations always wanted to leave this nation better than they had it, but this is now the first time in our nation's history when that can no longer be said. The generations to follow will not continue to have better lives than before because of the financial debt and moral decline in America.

Here's another: "Honor your mother and father." You know, that's one of the Ten Commandments. Please take notice that it does **not** say, "Honor your *perfect* mother and father." Your parents are not perfect, and neither are you. But the Lord expects us to honor our parents, and that seems to be going away to some degree.

These are just a few examples of how we are changing as a nation. There are many more, some of which I will continue to look at, but these are all part of an overall view of the state of the nation.

Now let me delve into why these things are happening. Again I go with the word of God because it's our plum line for truth. "Where there is no vision, the people perish" (Prov. 29:18 NKJV). The word *vision* means "spiritual sight."[9] Understand that when a nation loses their spiritual sight, it's only a matter of time before that nation will perish. That word *perish* means "to be destroyed."So, this verse really says: "When there is no longer spiritual sight, that nation will be destroyed." And that is what is happening in our nation today. We have lost our spiritual sight, and we are headed for destruction because of it.

This hasn't just happened overnight. The reason I said to look at the last fifty years is because that's about how long it's taken for this to evolve.

Here's the progression and the process of what's taking place. As I've mentioned before, when a nation begins to turn from God and act in rebellion to His word, He removes His hand of blessing and protection from that nation. It's a clear pattern through the Old Testament that when the nation of Israel would turn from God and act in rebellion against Him, things would not go well for the nation. Then, after a period of time, the people would repent and return to God, and things would go better for a time. This cycle repeated itself several times throughout the nation's history. They were and always have been God's chosen people, so when they repented, He would forgive them, and the blessings of God would flow again.

Now let's relate this to America. We were formed as a Christian nation. Some can debate that, but if you study our nation's history and our Founding Fathers,

---

[9] Miriam-Webster, 2023

you will see God's handwriting all over the founding of America.

The difference between America and Israel is that God chose Israel. Nowhere in the Bible is America mentioned by name. Does that not strike you as a bit odd considering we have been the most prosperous and powerful nation in the history of mankind? God has definitely blessed and protected us, but as we have turned from Him, a different dimension is taking place.

I want to use a word picture from the Bible as an illustration. Back in those days, towns and villages would build a wall for protection from potential enemies that would attack them. On the top of these walls, someone called a watchman would sit and peer into the distance, looking for any enemy approaching. I talked about this in a previous chapter, but it bears repeating. As an enemy would approach, the watchman would blow the warning trumpet to alert the people of an oncoming attack.

In relating this to America, at some point, we began to turn from God or to put it another way, we began to let down our spiritual wall of defense. Then we began to rebel against His Word, and this further let down our wall of defense. What occurred afterward was almost unnoticeable at first. While we let down our wall of defense, the enemy rode into camp undetected as if under the cover of night.

This came in the form of a moral revolution in the sixties that a small group of people with the intent of destroying our nation from within initiated. As I go through this process of these changes that have taken place in America, please grasp that Satan is the author behind all of this. It may seem extreme to give credit to the devil, but he is the author of chaos, division, hatred, depravity, and lawlessness. The sixties may have seemed to many a time of letting go and having fun, but it was the beginning of us as a nation going down the wrong road.

This small group of people who initiated and influenced the "'60's Revolution," as it has been named, knew exactly what they were doing and what they wanted to achieve. It began a moral revolution that continues to this day. They began in our universities and secured a solid foothold there.

I love the directness that God's word provides us about things. Read the following verse from the perspective of what takes place in our American universities. "Beware lest anyone cheat you through philosophy and empty deceit, according to the tradition of men, according to the basic principles of the world, and not according to Christ" (Col. 2:8 NKJV). That is **exactly** what is taking place to our young people in our universities. They go off to college, are not grounded and rooted in the word of God, then they sit and listen to liberal professors spew their belief system on them, and they become deceived. That's what Paul warned us about when he said, "Beware."

When this began in the sixties, those behind this knew it would take time. They would need to be patient. If you can remember, at that time, divorce was really frowned upon, much less the things that we now accept and celebrate. Who would have thought at that time that homosexuality would one day be celebrated and be the law of the land, that we would actually have a conversation about men using the women's bathroom was okay, or that people wanting to change their sex from male to female and vice versa would be accepted?

The latest trend is drag queens making appearances in our schools! It's mind-boggling to me that I even write some of these things. We now teach that these things are all part of being normal in the name of "tolerance" to our children in elementary schools. **Are you kidding?**

There is a section of Scripture that describes the decline of a nation of people that fits exactly what I'm describing here. This is the word of God, folks.

"The wrath of God is being revealed from heaven against all the godlessness and wickedness of people, who suppress the truth by their wickedness, since what may be known about God is plain to them. For since the creation of the world God's invisible qualities—His eternal power and divine nature—have been clearly seen, being understood from what has been made, so that people are without excuse. For although they knew God, they neither glorified Him as God nor gave thanks to Him, but their thinking became futile and their foolish hearts were darkened. Although they claimed to be wise, they became fools and exchanged the glory of the immortal God for images made to look like a mortal human being and birds and animals and reptiles.

Therefore God gave them over in the sinful desires of their hearts to sexual impurity for the degrading of their bodies with one another. They exchanged the truth about God for a lie, and worshiped and served created things rather than the Creator—who is forever praised. Amen. Because of this, God gave them over to shameful lusts. Even their women exchanged natural sexual relations for unnatural ones. In the same way the men also abandoned natural relations with women and were inflamed with lust for one another. Men committed shameful acts with other men, and received in themselves the due penalty for their error. Furthermore, just as they did not think it worthwhile to retain the knowledge of God, so God gave them over to a depraved mind, so that they do what ought not to be done. They have become filled with every kind of wickedness, evil, greed, and depravity. They are full of envy, murder, strife, deceit, and malice. They are gossips, slanderers, God-haters, insolent, arrogant, and boastful; they invent ways of doing evil; they disobey their parents; they have no understanding, no fidelity, no love, no mercy. Although they know God's righteous decree that those who do such things deserve death, they not only continue to do these very things but also approve of those who practice them (Rom. 1:18–32 NKJV).

I titled this book *You Can't Handle the Truth!* because of sections of Scripture like these. God's word doesn't candy-coat and gloss over our sinful nature. These verses in Romans describe the decline of a nation, and they describe our nation exactly. It talks about a nation that thinks it's wise, and then that nation begins to slide into sexual depravity to the point where its senses become dulled. That's what has happened in America. Our sense of right and wrong have become dull.

Here's another example of something that is destroying us but that didn't happen overnight. I remember, as many of you do, our parents or grandparents saying, "If you don't have the money for something, then don't buy it." At the end of the Ronald Reagan era, the national debt was $2.7 trillion. In 2023, the national debt is north of $32 trillion.[10][11] There was a time not that long ago that we in America had **zero** debt! **Zero debt**! Imagine that now. We have been a generous nation, and the Lord has blessed us in that area, but again, when a nation begins to turn from God, we begin to lose the gift of wisdom and discernment. It doesn't take a genius to know that you can't continue to spend money you don't have without some serious consequences. Yet in our nation today, we have continued to live in such a wasteful manner that we now look at the national debt and can't even imagine a way out.

---

[10] Debt.org, Timeline of U.S. Federal Debt Since Independence Day 1776

[11] Statista Research dept Aug7, 2023

These same people who are responsible for our moral decline are now in power in many ways. They have refused to have the courage and resolve to deal with our financial dilemma, but we the people are just as much to blame because we've elected these people over and over again. I recently read that as many as 65 percent of American families have less than $1000 in savings.[12] That is an astounding and frightening statistic.

As a nation, we have grown fat, lazy, and irresponsible. We are an arrogant nation that believes we can continue down this road without consequences. But folks, here me clearly. It simply can't continue without some kind of fiscal disaster happening.

There's really a simple answer to our financial situation. Here is what I believe we as a nation should do. First, we must tell all the nations that we give billions of dollars to that, for the time being, we will not be sending any more money to anyone. Period. We tell them that we must get our own house in order because if we fall, they all fall as well. We let them know that depending on how they respond to our decision will determine who gets funds when we start helping nations again.

Second, we **really** go line by line through our spending and cut the nonsense out. No more stupid wasteful spending. The only way to achieve this is by outlawing all special interest groups. **No more lobbyists!**

---

[12] FirstUnitedBank.com, Nearly 7 in 10 Americans have less than $1000 in Savings

Third, we limit political terms to two years. Let our elected officials understand that they are only there for two years, so the good old boy system is out. Many of our elected officials have been in office for decades and become entangled in the power and corruption that can breed in that environment. There is an atmosphere that exists in Washington with our politicians that seems to create an air of unaccountability. I believe we should let them serve for a short term and then they should return home to their elected areas.

Fourth, cut the corruption. If you get caught stealing from the people, you go to jail. You and I can't steal and get away with it, so why are the political leaders of our nation allowed to?

Fifth, it's time to go to work, people! Listen, I know that if you have a high school education, you may think you could be a rocket scientist, but you can't. There are jobs available, but we've created a welfare society where it's easier for some to collect a handout than it is to go get a job. What happened to something called **work ethic**? I will address this more in a later chapter.

These people I have been talking about who started this back in the sixties had this scenario in mind: The plan was to become a nation of people completely dependent on the government for everything, and we are getting dangerously close to being there.

Finally, I say it didn't happen overnight because of the behavior of the church. The church had been the catalyst God has used to push back the darkness throughout centuries in the past. The church was willing to take a stand for the things of God, but slowly, the church has been engulfed in greed, corruption, and more concerned with growth numbers than kingdom things. Pastors have watered down their messages because they didn't want to offend people in fear they would leave their church and go somewhere else. More concerned with the dollars coming into the church, the focus slowly shifted from biblical teaching and preaching to entertainment and appeasement. Oftentimes people don't really want to hear the truth of the Scriptures from the pulpit, and the Bible said it would be this way.

In 2 Timothy, Paul described what would take place in the last days: "For the time will come when they will not endure sound doctrine, but according to their own desires, because they have itching ears, they will heap up for themselves teachers; and they will turn their ears away from the truth, and be turned aside to fables" (2 Tim. 4:3–4 NKJV). These are the days we are living in right now. Paul said that people would eventually not "endure sound doctrine." *Endure* means to put up with; sound means wholesome, truthful; and *doctrine* means teaching.[13] So, Paul was saying that there would come a time where people would no longer "put up with wholesome, truthful teaching," but instead, because they have "itching ears," they would heap up teachers for themselves. People would find teachers who tell them what they want to hear. They would find preachers to tell them they can live their

---

[13] Miriam-Webster, 2023

lives any way they want, and God is all right with it. Paul said that they would "turn their ears away from the truth." That's why I decided to title this book *You Can't Handle the Truth!* People don't really want to hear the truth. They want to hear that everything is okay and will always be okay. And so the church has accommodated the people and have been silenced regarding the hard truth about things.

I can tell you this: our forefathers who came before us would be ashamed if they could see us now. If you don't believe me, just ask someone who's ninety to one hundred years old what they really think of America today and then just sit and listen.

We should be embarrassed that we've allowed this to happen.

We should be ashamed of the financial mess we've allowed ourselves to get into.

We should be ashamed of the disrespect for authority that we've allowed to take place in our society.

We should be disgusted by the moral depravity that is the new normal in America today.

We should be angry of how we have allowed our veterans to be treated.

We should be infuriated that we've allowed radical thinkers to hijack our educational institutions.

We should be ashamed that we've allowed over 50 million children to be slaughtered in the womb.

We should be outraged that we are laughed at around the world for what we've become.

We should be ashamed of the politicians that we've elected.

We should be ashamed of the condition of the church in America.

I could go on for quite a while longer.

We're all to blame for these things that are taking our nation down, but the sad fact is that most Americans aren't ashamed or upset because they either don't care, don't think they can change anything, or are just in denial.

You see, folks, this was all part of the plan of those few folks I talked about earlier. They were patient, intentional, and had a plan. And they knew it wouldn't happen overnight!

Chapter 6
Stop Your Whining

—ɱ—

We have become a nation of whiners! You know it. Can you ever remember a time when people would get offended like they do today? It's actually mind-boggling when you sit and listen to the news. Every day it seems there is another group offended by something that used to be normal everyday life.

Jesus said it would be this way in the very last days. He said, "And then many will be offended, will betray one another, and will hate one another" (Matt. 24:10 NKJV). You tell me, is that our world today?

I grew up in a different America than today. How many of you reading this remember this scene? I would begin to complain about something, and one of my parents would tell me to stop whining. I would continue, and then they would say this: "You want something to whine about? I'll give you something to whine about!" And almost always, the whining would cease immediately because I knew I was close to getting a spanking. And yet, we are a nation of people that whine and complain about almost everything.

Here is my opinion about why we've gotten to this place. (**If it offends you, you'll be okay!**) The Bible gives great counsel on raising children. Allow me to share a few verses with you. "He who spares his rod hates his son, but he who loves him disciplines him promptly" (Prov. 13:24 NKJV). Wow, this sounds like a good old fashion spanking. In our world today, many, if not most, people do not believe in spanking a child. So, let me ask a stupid question here. Are we then to assume that God got this wrong here in Proverbs? I challenge you that many of our problems in society today stem from a lack of discipline somewhere along the way. (**I told you that many would be offended.**)

Here's another verse: "Do not withhold correction from a child, for if you beat him with a rod, he will not die. [I can give testimony to this.] You shall beat him with a rod, and deliver his soul from hell" (Prov. 23:13 NKJV). You may think this sounds a lot like child abuse, but I call it the word of God.

We all need disciplining from time to time, and children must learn from being disciplined. You may say, "Craig, I strongly disagree with you about this." Okay, but take a look at our nation. The level of disrespect for any kind of authority is astounding. Complaining has become an art form. Most people believe that if they complain loud enough and long enough, they will eventually get their way, and unfortunately, most of the time, they're right.

Here's another verse: "The rod and rebuke give wisdom, but a child left to himself brings shame to his mother" (Prov. 29:15 NKJV).

With all due respect, children don't know what's best for them, and as adults, we must train them and discipline them to know right from wrong. If we don't, the result is a society that eventually grows up undisciplined and believes they can whine and throw temper tantrums whenever they want and get their way. Does this sound familiar to anyone other than me?

There are many more verses about discipline in the Bible, but here's my point with all this. When we as a nation of people turn from God and His word, so many things begin to go wrong. Even as adults, we need discipline. Another of my life verse is: "My son, do not despise the chastening of the LORD, nor detest His correction; for whom the LORD loves He corrects" (Prov. 3:11–12 NKJV). Sometimes in my life, even as an adult, I need the correction that the word of God brings.

Here's a wild thought: Can you imagine if we had to bring back the draft in this country? For all you young people out there, the word *draft* hasn't always referred to beer. But think about it. What would be the response if we suddenly said, "Listen, we need all young people out of high school to enlist in the Armed Services for two years." By the way, do you know that many countries around the world do this exact thing?[14]

Can you imagine the response here in America? "No cell phones needed. We'll cut your hair when you get here. Just come on in for two years of service."

---

[14] Wikipedia.org, List of Enlistment age by Country

There would be massive protests on campuses around the nation, saying, "You can't do this. We don't deserve this. We're not going to allow this to happen."

I repeat, we have become a nation of whiners!

In the Old Testament, when the nation complained about God over and over again, He eventually decided to allow that whole generation to wander in the wilderness for forty years when the promised land was only an eleven-day journey.[15] God does not like it when we complain and whine about things. Philippians 2:14–15 NKJV says, "Do all things without complaining and disputing, that you may become blameless and harmless, children of God, without fault in the midst of a crooked and perverse generation, among whom you shine as lights in the world."

Now, let me be the first to confess that I sometimes find myself complaining and have to check myself. We must be very careful because, at some point, we can acquire a "complaining spirit." God hates it when His children complain about things here on earth because, ultimately, it doesn't really matter. We're just passing through this world, and God wants us to be mindful of that fact.

Folks, if you've ever listened to my radio show, then you know I sincerely believe that we are living in the very last days before the return of Jesus Christ. Does that mean two years, twenty years, fifty years . . . No one, I repeat, **no one** knows that answer; however, the Bible gives us many conditions that will be prevalent

---

[15] Exodus NKJV

in our world just before the return of Jesus, and these signs are **everywhere**.

I believe the devil is using a whining spirit in our country as part of his scheme to divide and ultimately destroy us. A whining spirit is really a self-centered spirit. When we whine and complain about things, we are basically saying that we want our way, and if we don't get our way, we are going to yell, scream, push, and make a scene until we get our way.

There is a certain method the progressives use that exhibits this whining. You can see it at work whenever they are on a program with anyone with an opposing viewpoint from theirs. They make a point to talk over the other person, interrupt the other person, and get louder if need be, until the other person is silenced. That is the tactic they use to silence someone with an opinion different than their own.

These are a minority of people who are attempting to drag us down as a nation because they yell louder, are relentless, and know that they can silence us if they are persistent enough. They are pawns for the devil, and most of them don't even know it. They are being deceived, which is another one of the signs that we are in the very last days. Paul tells us in 2 Timothy 3:13 NKJV: "But evil men and imposters will grow worse and worse, deceiving and being deceived." That word *imposters* means "seducers" in the original Greek language.[16] That means people will come on the scene who will seduce others into their way of

---

[16] Miriam-Webster, 2023

thinking. They themselves have been deceived and now they are deceiving others. This is exactly what is taking place in our nation today.

Ladies and gentlemen, we no longer have the luxury of kicking the can down the road. We are at a point when we **must** confront these issues and deal with them before it's too late if we're not there already. I pray that you can feel my heartbeat and that I love my country, but I don't recognize the great country I grew up in. We are in a battle for the fabric of America, and I am trying to be obedient to the calling God has put on me to speak up and speak the truth. Sometimes the truth hurts. I get that. I really do. But I am genuinely trying to sound a warning here that I feel the Lord is leading me to do. Jesus Christ is my Lord and Savior! And I will never put anything before Him, including my country, but I love America and care enough to speak out.

Chapter 7
Count Your Blessings

—⁓—

Perspective is so important in life. A great example is a glass that is half full. One person says the glass is half full, while someone else says it's half empty. Then a third person may even say the glass is full, with half fluid and the other half air. That is three different people with three different perspectives on the same glass.

I find it curious that a percentage of the population believes that living in America is a blessing and that this is by far the greatest country in the world. A second group is lukewarm about America and doesn't have much of an opinion about whether this is a great country or not. Then there is a third group that believes we are a horrible country, and they want to destroy it. Again, it is three different perspectives on the same topic.

Let's examine each of these groups' perspectives on America.

First, let's look at Group #1. This is the group that believes that living in America is a blessing and that this is by far the greatest country in the world. In my opinion, this group, to a large degree, are God-fearing Christians. Most people who confess Jesus as their Lord and Savior love America and will tell you so. They also realize that God has blessed America tremendously. Psalm 33:12 NKJV says, "Blessed is the nation whose God is the LORD. The people He has chosen as His own inheritance." The Scripture is very clear. The nation whose God is the Lord is a blessed nation.

These people in the first group I'm describing **know** that America is a blessed nation and where those blessings come from. This group is also very family oriented; they believe in honoring our military men and women, and they support law and order and those police officers who put their lives on the line daily to protect and serve our communities.

Here is the challenge for the first group I am describing. **Have we taken these blessings for granted?** Stop and think about that statement for a few minutes. How many of us in that group can honestly say that we haven't? I can't honestly say that I don't take some of God's blessings for granted. Can you?

It's easy to thank Him at Thanksgiving, Christmas, or when something spectacular happens in our lives, but how about **all** things like the freedom to worship, the freedom of speech that we have enjoyed throughout our nation's history, the beautiful country He has blessed us with, clean water, clean air, the simple act of being able to travel whenever and wherever we want, our military men and women, our police officers and firefighters, our elderly loved ones . . . I can go on and on.

Am I grateful for these things? Yes. But do I stop very often and **really** spend time thinking about all these and so many more things God does for me and my family? In truth, I don't do it enough. And if I'm being honest, I admit that I take many of the blessings of God for granted. Can I get a witness from anyone else this applies to? Jesus spoke to this in Revelation 2:2–5 NKJV in speaking to one of the seven churches when He said:

> "I know your works, your labor, your patience, and that you cannot bear those that are evil. And you have tested those who say they are apostles and are not, and have found them to be liars; and you have preserved and have patience, and have labored for My name's sake and have not become weary. Nevertheless I have this against you, that you have left your first love. Remember therefore from where you have fallen; repent and do the first works, or else I will come to you quickly and remove your lampstand from its place—unless you repent."

These are **very** sobering words from Jesus. This church or group had some good traits, but they had lost their first love. These people I am referring to in Group #1 love America and love Jesus, but I believe those of us in this group have to ask ourselves this question: **Have we lost our first love?** I believe many would say no.

Allow me to share another Scripture with you. In Jude, the writer says in verse 3 NKJV: "Beloved [he is speaking to fellow believers], while I was very diligent to write to you concerning our common salvation, I found it necessary to write to you exhorting you to contend earnestly for the faith which was once for all delivered to the saints." The words *contend earnestly* in the original Greek language is the word *epagonizomai*, and it means "to struggle for" something.[17]

To this first group, here is another question: Have we grown silent in the struggle for the faith here in America? Do we now just stay silent and go along with society and the changes that we **know** are against what God says about right and wrong, about this moral depravity that is destroying our nation? If those of us in this group who are supposed to be the "defenders of the faith" have gone silent, then why is it surprising that we are in the situation we now find ourselves in America?

Again, if we, the supposed defenders of the faith, have gone silent when the Bible clearly tells us to "contend earnestly" for the faith, have we not disobeyed God and His Word? Show me where it says in the Bible that we shouldn't share our faith. Show me where in the Bible it tells us to just go along with whatever the current society says is popular. Show me in the Bible where it says to compromise our morals and values to pacify the masses. You can't show me that because the Bible doesn't tell us to do that.

---

[17] Strong's Concordance

Jesus told us that we are called to be "salt and light." In Matthew, Jesus said:

> "You are the salt of the earth; but if the salt loses its flavor, how shall it be seasoned? It is then good for nothing but to be thrown out and trampled underfoot by men. You are the light of the world. A city that is set on a hill cannot be hidden. Nor do they light a lamp and put it under a basket, but on a lampstand, and it gives light to all who are in the house. Let your light so shine before men, that they may see your good works and glorify your Father in heaven" (Matt. 5:13-16 NKJV).

If we aren't the salt and light that Jesus told us to be, this is **turning away from God and His word!** This is all in reference to Group #1 that loves Jesus and America.

Now, let's examine Group #2. Remember, this group is lukewarm and doesn't have much of an opinion about whether America is a great country or not.

These are people who just want to go through life, do their own thing, and don't want to offend anyone or be judgmental toward anyone. They tend to stick to the middle of the road and don't really take a stand for much. The mentality here is, "Who are you to judge me about anything?" They believe that just because you believe something is true doesn't mean they believe it. Truth is relevant to whatever they want it to be. Their attitude is, "You do and believe what you want, and

I'll do the same, but don't try to convince me of your viewpoint."

This is also the fastest-growing sector of the population in America, referred to as "Nones." They really don't have any religious or spiritual beliefs. Asked about their religious affiliation, they simply answer, "None."

At this point, I will tell you that I struggle with some of the things I hear and see regarding this group. I believe this is the group that has been deceived the deepest. They will tell you that they are "basically good people." Yet, my Bible says, "As it is written: 'There is none righteous, no, not one; There is none who understands; There is none who seeks after God. They have all turned aside; They have together become unprofitable; There is none who does good, no, not one'" (Rom. 3:10–12 NKJV). Notice that these verses apply to everyone.

One of the differences between Group #1 and Group #2 is that those in Group #1 (for the most part) understand that they have "all sinned and fallen short of the glory of God, being justified freely by His grace through the redemption that is in Christ Jesus" (Rom. 3:23–24 NKJV). Knowing this creates the statement I made about the first group that they believe America is a great nation that has been blessed and know where those blessings come from.

I don't believe Group #2 really grasps the benefits that God has bestowed on America, or they really don't care. While definitely taking these blessings for granted, they also don't have a grasp on or appreciate the sacrifices past generations have made throughout our nation's history.

When I talk about the sacrifices made for what we have and enjoy in America, of course I am referring to the men and women who have served in the armed forces for our freedoms, and not only those who directly served but also their immediate and extended families as well. When I thank a veteran for their service, if they are with their spouse, I thank that person as well because, in my opinion, that person served as well. They sacrificed a tremendous amount right along with the actual service member. We should **all be very grateful** for these families who have gone into battle to defend our nation.

I am not only referring to the military families but the men and women in blue and firefighters who guard and protect us day in and day out so we can go about our daily lives, knowing that we live in the greatest country in the world.

I think many of those in Group #2 have mixed feelings about all these people who have and continue to protect and serve us here at home. I know many people who supported de-funding the police in the last few years, and this astounds me. My response the first time I heard the idea was, "Who thinks this is a good idea?" The fact that we live in a country that has been known for standing up for law and order, and we now have people who don't understand or seem to care about the importance of that really saddens me. I also believe this is one of the areas of deception taking place in our nation today. There are **major** consequences to these choices we are making as a nation right now.

The devil is very busy at work to destroy America and the increase in lawlessness is one of the tactics he is using. Jesus actually said it would be this way in the very last days before His return in Matthew when He said: "And then many will be offended, will betray one another, and will hate one another. Then many false prophets will rise up and deceive many. And because lawlessness will abound, the love of many will grow cold" (Matt. 24:10–12 NKJV). Don't these words from Jesus sound exactly like what is taking place in America today?

I also want make mention of our parents, grandparents and generations that came before us. Today we are living in a time of unprecedented wealth, prosperity, and comfort. We don't think we could lose this, but it's happening before our very eyes. The generations before us had much more difficult lives than we do today, and they worked **extremely** hard for us to have the life we now have.

In the past, every generation made it part of their generation's duty to leave America a better place than what it was in their time. It grieves me to make this statement, but this will be the first time in our nation's history that we can't say that. My generation cannot truthfully say that we are leaving America in a better place than our parents left for us.

At the writing of this book, I am in my sixties, and in my opinion, my generation has dropped the ball in this area. There are a few major reasons for this. First,

I challenge you to ask one hundred people where the spiritual influence came from in their lives, and most will say, "My mother or grandmother." Men, that's not the way God intended it to be! Where are the men of God who are so badly needed in America at this moment in our history?

Listen to these sobering words spoken by the Lord through Jeremiah the prophet in warning the nation to repent and return to Him:

> "Now therefore, speak to the MEN of Judah and to the inhabitants of Jerusalem, saying, "Thus says the Lord: 'Behold, I am fashioning a disaster and devising a plan against you. Return now every one from his evil way, and make your ways and your doings good.'" And they said, "That is hopeless! So we will walk according to our own plans, and we will every one obey the dictates of his evil heart" (Jer. 18:11–12 NKJV).

In case you wonder about the man's role in the family, here is what God's Word says: "For the husband is head of the wife, as also Christ is head of the church; and He is the Savior of the body. Therefore, just as the church is subject to Christ, so let the wives be to their own husbands in everything. Husbands, love your wives, just as Christ also loved the church and gave Himself for her, that He might sanctify and cleanse her with the washing of water by the word, that He might present her to Himself a glorious church, not having spot or wrinkle or any such thing, but that she should be holy and without blemish. So husbands ought to love their own wives as their own bodies; he who loves his wife loves himself. For no one ever hated his own flesh, but nourishes and cherishes it, just as the Lord does the church. For we are members of His body, of His flesh and of His bones. "For this reason a man shall leave his father and mother and be joined to his wife, and the two shall become one flesh" (Eph. 5:23–31 NKJV).

You may think this is outdated and no longer relevant in our world today, but I would like you to remember that it is the word of the living God. In the verses above, the devil has perverted the meaning to say that women are somehow inferior or below men. That is **absolutely not what these verses mean**.

The first thing to keep in mind is that God is a God of order. He is not the author of chaos and confusion. God has an order He has set in place, and that order is perfect. The devil wants to attack that order and does it by questioning it or perverting it. The devil is smart and cunning. Many times, instead of completely opposing God's order, he will just pervert it. He's subtle, so it may not seem as though it's open rebellion to God.

Over a period of time, the man's role in the family and in this nation greatly diminished. Spiritually, to a large degree, men have become silenced about their faith. This silence has had a tremendous negative affect on the family and society.

The media have mocked and denigrated men in general, and there is now a negative connotation surrounding the image of what men should be in the family and our society.

I have asked this question many times of men: "Do you spend quality time praying for your wife, your family, and this nation?" As men, we should be the spiritual leaders for our families, but unfortunately, for too long, that has not been the case. If there has ever been a time in this nation's history where men are needed to provide spiritual strength and leadership, it's now!

The other area of perversion the devil has created concerning the family is the structure of one man and one woman joining together to become one. God created the family. And as I said, God is a God of order. He knows what's best for us. So in his attempt to change and destroy the family, Satan is attacking one of the most important structures that God put in place.

As I mentioned before, I believe that we have lost our spiritual way in America, and the dismantling of the family as God intended it to be will prove to be one of the biggest reasons for the downfall of our nation.

Those in Group #2 have become unaware or numb to the effects of the changing family structure from what God intended it to be. In reality, I believe most in this group either simply don't care about what I'm talking about or have been deceived to the point that they are just going along with whatever the world says is right and wrong and don't want to take a stand against what society decides to do.

Then there is Group #3. This group is the very loud, very aggressive minority that hates America and would like to see it destroyed. I believe this group looks down their nose at those of us who believe in God and **really** detest those of us who speak up about Jesus Christ. They either have no idea or don't care about the sacrifices that previous generations have made for this country. They see all the things that are wrong with America and want it all to be burned down.

I've often wondered about this group. Have they ever been to a third-world country and witnessed what life is like there? Is this really the nation that they want America to become?

The word *socialism* has been thrown around and become popular, but most people have no idea what it really means. Can anyone please show me a socialist country that has proved to be a successful model for a nation?

We have all seen before-and-after pictures of something, and the after picture is always so much better than the before. I have asked people in this group to please paint me a picture of what the *after* will look like in America, and nobody can give me an accurate description.

I know what the *before* picture is, and despite the faults of America, it has been proven to be the greatest, most free, most prosperous nation in the history of mankind. We have privileges here that other nations dream about. Why is it that people from all over the world still want to come to America? And here is a very simple question for people in this group: If you hate this nation, then why don't you decide where else you would like to live in this world and simply move there?

Those in this group would like to see the fabric of our nation completely destroyed.

If those of us in Group #1 and Group #2 remain silent, then those in Group #3 will prevail, and the country that so many of us love and have taken for granted will be destroyed.

I sincerely believe that we are at a tipping point in our nation's history.

We have been so blessed by God! But I believe it is naïve to think these blessings can't be removed. In Jeremiah 18, it says:

> "Then the word of the Lord came to me, saying: "O house of Israel, can I not do with you as this potter?" says the Lord. "Look, as the clay is in the potter's hand, so are you in My hand, O house of Israel! The instant I speak concerning a nation and concerning a kingdom, to pluck up, to pull down, and to destroy it, if that nation against whom I have spoken turns from its evil, I will relent of the disaster that I thought to bring upon it. And the instant I speak concerning a nation and concerning a kingdom, to build and to plant it, if it does evil in My sight so that it does not obey My voice, then I will relent concerning the good with which I said I would benefit it" (Jer. 18:5–10 NKJV).

God says here that nations are in His hand. This is very clear Scripture about a nation that either repents and turns from evil or continues to disobey the word of God and brings the judgement of God upon itself.

At some point, and we may already be there, the judgment of God will fall upon America.

The truth of God's Word will stand forever. He can build up or destroy a nation. My great concern is that because of the decisions we are making and allowing to be made, at some point, we will bring the judgment of God upon America!

Chapter 8

What Do You Mean "Work Ethic"?

—◊◊◊—

I remember when I was a young teenager, I asked my father for a new pair of basketball shoes. He said, "Let's go," so we got in the car, and he drove me to a local barbecue restaurant, walked me inside, asked for the manager, and told that manager that I wanted a job busing tables and washing dishes. I was shocked. I thought we were going to buy some new basketball shoes, but instead, my father introduced me to the world of "if you want something, go work for it."

From an early age, all the kids in our family were taught a very strong work ethic. We all started working as young teenagers. I remember my mother working long hours and then coming home and taking care of the family. A strong work ethic was ingrained in all four of us kids. To this day, I still have that work ethic my parents instilled in me. Like many of you reading this book, it really frustrates me as I witness the laziness and entitlement mentality that has developed in America.

There are so many things that a strong work ethic does for a young person. First, it helps them to understand the value of a dollar. I think many young people today do not understand how much things really cost, how much effort it takes to get that much money, and because of that, they don't appreciate the things that have been provided for them.

Recently, my grandson got a job, and when he got his first paycheck, he was shocked how much he had to pay in taxes and what he netted after deductions. I am also sure that he thinks differently about what he decides to spend his hard-earned money on now and in the future. This was his first lesson on the value of a dollar.

Another benefit of a strong work ethic is that it instills respect for authority. I am blessed that I own my own company, but for a large portion of my life, I worked for other people. Like most of you, I had a boss, and I learned to respect my boss, even if sometimes I didn't agree with him or her. I am taken back at the level of disrespect I witness in the world today and believe the lack of work ethic has contributed to this.

The Bible has something to say about this in Romans: "Let every soul be subject to the governing authorities. For there is no authority except from God, and the authorities that exist are appointed by God" (Rom. 13:1 NKJV). This can apply to the government as well as the workplace. We may not agree with those in a position of authority over us, but we are to respect them. I may not agree with how my government spends my tax dollars, but I still have to pay my taxes. This is just one example of respecting authority.

Another great aspect of a strong work ethic is that it creates self-worth and self-value in a person. One of the things that happened during covid was that so many people became dependent on the government and got used to accepting a handout from the government. These people have been deceived into believing that it's okay to stay at home, not work, and pick up a check.

This is a very dangerous mindset for several reasons. First, it gives the government too much control of people's lives. Secondly, when people don't work, over a period of time, they begin to lose their identity and purpose in life. That's one of the reasons the suicide rate spiked during covid. People began to lose their self-worth and slipped into a depression. I think there was a very sinister element to the "handouts" during covid, and the effects are still being felt.

There is another benefit of a strong worth ethic, and it's that God honors hard work. In 2 Thessalonians, Paul addresses this:

"But we command you, brethren, in the name of our Lord Jesus Christ, that you withdraw from every brother who walks disorderly and not according to the tradition which he received from us. For you yourselves know how you ought to follow us, for we were not disorderly among you; nor did we eat anyone's bread free of charge, but worked with labor and toil night and day,

that we might not be a burden to any of you,
not because we do not have authority, but to
make ourselves an example of how you should
follow us. For even when we were with you, we
commanded you this: If anyone will not work,
neither shall he eat" (2 Thess. 3:6–10 NKJV).

Paul states here that we shouldn't be a burden to
others if we have the capability to work.

Do people really think that taking a handout from
the government won't cost us anything? Someone has
to pay for all these programs and free stuff. Future
generations will suffer the consequences of the decisions that are being made today.

At some point, those who are able to work but don't
want to are actually stealing from those who are
working. In Ephesians, the Bible says, "Let him who
stole steal no longer, but rather let him labor, working
with his hands what is good, that he may have something to give him who has need" (Eph. 4:28 NKJV).

We are called to work, so then we can be generous
and help those who are **really in need** and also be
able to provide for our own families.

The Bible actually has quite a bit to say about the
subject of work. Here is another verse that speaks
about working to be able to provide. "But if anyone
does not provide for his own, and especially for those
of his household, he has denied the faith and is worse
than an unbeliever" (1 Tim. 5:8 NKJV). The Lord
expects us to work if we are able to.

One more Scripture I want to share with you comes from Colossians: "And whatever you do in word or deed, do all in the name of the Lord Jesus, giving thanks to God the Father through Him" (Col. 3:17 NKJV).

That word *deed* in the original Greek is the word *ergon*, and it means "to work." God says we should work "in the name of the Lord Jesus" and give thanks to God for the opportunity.

It's easy to understand all the benefits of a strong work ethic. Americans used to have one of the strongest work ethics in the world, but it's no longer the case. The rest of the world is either catching up to us or surpassing us in this area.

We see this clearly in the area of students. America ranks very poorly in the area of academics.[18] Students from around the world have a very strong work ethic in the area of education because they want to improve their lives and understand it takes hard work.

Another very important benefit of a strong work ethic is that it creates discipline. This is a topic that isn't discussed much in today's world, but it's extremely important.

A disciplined life has order to it. It has structure. Think about it. A person with a strong work ethic needs to be up at a certain time, which means they also must go to bed at a certain time. They get in a certain routine on a daily basis, which helps to create positive habits. There is a purpose for them. They must be at work at a certain time, so they must be responsible

---

[18] Amadeo, "U.S. Education Rankings Are Falling Behind the Rest of the World",

about their time. They have certain responsibilities at their job that they must perform. They are expected to get things done in a timely manner and with a certain level of competence. When they do things well and excel at their job, oftentimes, it leads to being promoted to a higher position.

If you examine people who are very successful in their lives, most of the time, one of the common denominators is a strong work ethic. If you ask them why and how they became successful, more times than not, they will tell you that they worked hard to get where they are at. I can tell you from experience that I have been promoted over smarter people in my life because I simply outworked them. As I've said, a disciplined life is an ordered life, and God is a God of order. A disciplined life honors God.

We see this in the military. Look at the life of anyone who has been in the military, and you will see a disciplined life. The military teaches discipline, and it teaches excellence. The American armed forces have always been known for its excellence, discipline, and hard work. That's what has helped to make it the great military force that it has been throughout our nation's history, but that seems to be changing.

Americans used to be known for our work ethic. It was part of who we were, and the rest of the world knew it, but that has changed over the last several years. It was part of the fabric of this nation. I really believe that we, as a nation, have begun to lose our competitive edge in the world, and it's largely due to the loss of our strong work ethic that we have always had.

Along with losing our competitive edge comes the loss of respect from other nations around the world. For the last two hundred years, other nations respected us, feared us, and wanted to be like us. America had the respect and reputation of being the greatest nation on earth. Let me ask you a very candid question: Has that begun to change? Are we still considered the greatest nation on earth? Do other nations still respect us as they used to?

I believe that other nations around the world are watching America today and are wondering what is going on here. We have been the most blessed nation in the history of mankind, and it appears that we are squandering our blessings. Look around us. We see it in **so many ways**. It really grieves me to watch what is taking place in my nation today.

As our morals, values, and strong work ethic continue to diminish, we are witnessing our standard of living slipping as well. This is a **very serious time** in our nation's history, and I am concerned that many people are either oblivious to it or have lost the desire for the excellence we once had.

The blessings we have enjoyed from God are not guaranteed. They must be treasured, protected, and not be taken for granted. I want to encourage all believers in Christ to be in prayer for America at this current time because if we lose what God has blessed us with, we may not be able to recapture it again. I have children and grandchildren, as many of you do, and I am very concerned with what the nation will look like in the future. As we continue to turn from God, if

He removes His hand of blessing and protection from us, then America as we know it will cease to exist.

I want to leave you with a Scripture that the Lord has put on my heart. Please think about these verses regarding America today:

> "'If you will return, O Israel,' says the Lord, 'Return to Me; And if you will put away your abominations out of My sight, Then you shall not be moved. And you shall swear, "The Lord lives," In truth, in judgment, and in righteousness; The nations shall bless themselves in Him, And in Him they shall glory'" (Jer. 4:1–2 NKJV).

Now substitute America for Israel. America . . . hear the word of the Lord!

Chapter 9
The Entitlement Era

—ꝏ—

H ere is how Webster defines *entitlement*:

noun
en• ti• tle• ment | \ in-ˈtī-tᵊl-mənt , en- \
Definition:
1a : the state or condition of being entitled
2: belief that one is deserving of or entitled to certain
privileges
3: a government program providing benefits to members of a
specified group[19]

"We are also the so-called entitled generation, ... told by helicopter parents and the media, from the moment we exited the womb, that we could be "whatever we wanted"— Jessica Bennett and Jesse Ellison. [20]

We are now living in an **era of entitlement** in America.

In this chapter, we will examine this phenomenon that now exists in our nation. We are a culture that

---

[19] Miriam-Webster, 2023
[20] News Week June 11, 2010

feels as though we "deserve" certain things for no apparent reason.

I would like to make comments about each of these three definitions from Webster and also examine what God's word says about this subject.

Let's start with definition #1: "the state or condition of being entitled." What may have started out as an exception from time to time or an act of a very small child has grown into a national pastime. There is a significant percentage of Americans who now feel as though they are entitled to things and privileges that have never been granted to people in our nation's history. This group has become conditioned to feel this way, but many of us are scratching our heads and thinking, "Are these people crazy?"

Definition #2: "Belief that one is deserving of or entitled to certain privileges." How have we gotten to the place where some people think they deserve to take from others what is not theirs to take or that they are "owed" something they haven't earned? This is a really dangerous condition in our country today. This creates such a division among people when some think they deserve certain privileges that others in our nation don't deserve.

The devil is using this mentality to divide America in many ways. I know many people of different classes and races who are doing very well in life, and I also know many people of different classes and races who struggle. I grew up in a time and country that it was understood that we got what we worked for. If you wanted to be successful bad enough and had the work ethic it took to make it, you would eventually become successful.

I am grateful that my parents instilled in me a strong work ethic that has served me well in my life, but if I was lazy or thought that things should be handed to me because I deserved them, I would not be where I am today.

The real truth is that we should **all be grateful** that we don't get what we deserve. Many times in my prayers, I say, "Lord, thank You for not giving me what I deserve. I asked for Your mercy and Your grace. In Jesus's name. Amen!"

Truth be told, if we got what we deserved, we would all be in hell.

Here's what the Bible says: Isaiah 64:6 NKJV "But we are all like an unclean thing, and all our righteousness's are like filthy rags."

The Word of God can be so direct sometimes that we are almost taken back by it. Here in Isaiah, the Word states that what we think of ourselves concerning how righteous we are is disgusting. We all know what a pile of filthy rags looks like, and that is exactly what God says our righteousness is to Him. Can you imagine standing before God and telling Him why you deserve this or that?

Job tried that, and when he questioned God, here was God's response to Job: "Then the LORD answered Job out of the whirlwind and said: 'Who is this who darkens counsel by words without knowledge? Now prepare yourself like a man; I will question you, and you shall answer Me'" (Job 38:1–3 NKJV).

Just stop and try to imagine yourself in Job's position here; talk about a bad day! God proceeds to ask Job a series of questions that Job has no answer for, and it becomes very quick to Job that he has been sadly mistaken about his own self-righteousness. God starts out in verse 4 with: "Where were you when I laid the foundations of the earth? Tell Me if you have understanding." In Job 38:12 NKJV God says, "Have you commanded the morning since your days began, and caused the dawn to know its place?"

Job's first response to a long list of questions from God is: "Behold, I am vile; what's shall I answer You? I lay my hand over my mouth." Job is confronted with the stark reality that he is **way out of line** and that any righteousness he thinks of himself is wildly misplaced!

I invite you to go read Job 38–42. For anyone who believes they are deserving or entitled to something, this section of Scripture will present a completely different perspective.

Romans 3:10 NKJV says, "There is none righteous, no, not one." Any questions about that verse?

The devil has done a masterful job of telling people that they are somehow entitled to and deserve things that they either haven't worked for or that they can take from others who **have** worked for them.

As for work ethic, the Bible states in 2 Thessalonians 3:10 NKJV, "If anyone will not work, neither shall he eat." This is an astounding statement! Basically, it says that if someone is able to work, then they should work. This doesn't include those who can't work because of an illness or retired people. Retired people have worked most of their lives and now get to enjoy the fruit of their labors.

Those who have a real sickness that won't enable them to work should be cared for by those of us who can work, but the mindset that has taken hold in America is that there are some who don't **want** to work and **want** to take advantage of the government (which means they are taking advantage of those who **do** work) is just crazy.

In conclusion, America became a great nation because God has tremendously blessed us but also because we have always had a great work ethic and have been willing to work harder than others around the world. This has now changed, and we are falling behind other nations that don't have the entitlement attitude, and they are outworking us. Because of this, we are losing our status as the greatest nation in the world, and the consequences will be extremely dire.

If you don't think we can lose what we have been blessed with as a nation, you are wrong. My concern is that future American generations have no idea what is taking place, and when the lights finally come on, it will be too late. The freedoms that our forefathers worked so hard for are being squandered before our very own eyes, and if we don't wake up to this fact very soon, we will lose these freedoms!

Chapter 10
Respect for Your Elders

—ɯ—

This is a phrase most of us heard when we were growing up, but somewhere along the way, it has disappeared, and if you say it now, chances are you will get the proverbial rolling of the eyes.

Respect for your elders has been and still is a very important concept that is being mocked and lost in America today, but I want to address it in this chapter.

There was a time before all the technology and social media that people would sit and actually talk to each other. I don't just mean casual talking in the sense of two or three friends sitting around with their phones in their hands but a time when people would spend an entire evening or a weekend afternoon without any outside technology and really talk about things.

These were times when one generation might tell the younger generation about past relatives, historical events that had taken place that were important in our nation's history, or discuss values, morals, and beliefs that were important to families and communities. This was an opportunity time for the elders in a family to impart wisdom into the next generation, and these times would also bring families closer together and endear the older members of the family to the younger generation.

This may appear to be an insignificant concept, but I can assure you that's not the case. Many of us have very fond memories of those who have gone before us, and the times of sitting and visiting together are priceless.

One of the devil's tools and a tactic of those who seek to destroy America is to tear down the family and weaken the bonds that exist from generation to generation.

When I was growing up, I was taught to be respectful of those who were older than I was, be polite to others older than myself, and **never** to talk back (or "sass," as it was called) to an adult. The word *sass* actually means "to be rude" or "disrespectful."[21]

That sounds so foreign in our world today. We now live in a society where respect for your elders is laughed at, and that's the reason that we witness so much chaos in our schools. Again, not to date myself, but when I was in school, there was no such thing as talking back to teachers in the classroom. We were to listen to and behave for our teachers, and if we didn't, there were severe consequences. The thought of arguing with, disrespecting, and challenging a teacher was grounds for discipline or suspension, and we would **never** have thought of actually having an

---

[21] Miriam-Webster, 2023

altercation with a faculty member without expecting to be expelled from school.

When I see young people becoming violent in classrooms toward teachers, it shocks and really saddens me that we have gotten to this point as a society where we will tolerate such behavior. Many of us have experienced getting "licks," as they were called, when I grew up at school by a principal or a coach for things we did that went against certain rules we were expected to abide by.

This disrespect for elders and authority begins at home. When we stopped disciplining our children at home is when things began to change. I'm certainly not for beating or abusing children in any form or fashion, but when I was disrespectful to elders, teachers, or those in authority, I **knew** I was going to get some type of physical discipline when I got home.

The Bible states in several places that we should discipline our children. I understand that this is a very sensitive subject in our world today.

I encourage you to examine people who are disciplined in their lives as adults, and the majority of them will tell you that they experienced being disciplined as a child.

*Please don't confuse spanking with beating. It's **never** okay to beat a child, but children who know they will receive discipline if they misbehave are much better-behaved children.

When we look at the topic of respect for your elders, there's another aspect of it worth mentioning. If you examine many cultures that have existed for centuries

longer than America, one of the common character-
istics is that they love, endear, respect, and take care
of their elderly population.

Growing up, I was blessed to have one of my grand-
mothers living with us for most of my childhood, and
there were so many blessings tied to that. First, I got
to spend a tremendous amount of time with my grandmother. I believe almost everyone loves their grand-
mothers, so imagine Grandma always being around
as a small child. It was also a huge blessing to her
because she got to spend a tremendous amount of time
with all four of her grandkids. It was a great blessing
to my parents because if they needed to or wanted to
go somewhere, they never had to worry because us
kids were with our grandmother. They had a full-time
babysitter! And I was able to witness the love my parents showed to the generation before them.

Were there sacrifices my parents made to take care
of my grandmother? Yes, but those sacrifices were
greatly outweighed by the blessing of having an elderly
relative in the house. To this day, I have so many fond
memories of my grandmother living with us, and I am
so grateful that my parents took her in to live with us.

Today, we are so busy, so stressed, and so dis-
tracted by many things that we have neglected many
of our elderly. Micah and I have visited senior facilities
many times, and it is heartbreaking to hear that many
of the residents were dropped off, and their families
seldom, if ever, come and visit them.

There are nations that take care of their elderly
loved ones by taking them in and caring for them, and

it says so much about that society. We used to do that to a large degree here in America, but it doesn't seem to be as prevalent today as it once was. I sincerely believe when a nation stops caring for the elderly and stops respecting the elderly, that nation is headed down a very disturbing path.

In 1 Timothy 5:8 NKJV, the Scripture says, "If anyone does not provide for his own, and especially for those of his household, he has denied the faith and is worse off than an unbeliever." It also says in Proverbs 23:22 NKJV, "Listen to your father who gave you life, and do not despise your mother when she is old." God expects us to care for the elderly, and when the respect for our elders no longer exists, we as a nation are in a sad state.

Chapter 11

Corruption, Corruption, Corruption!

—ɯɯ—

I could write an entire book about this chapter because it's that important and that rampant in America today!

As I was preparing to write this chapter, I thought, "Where do I even start?" Let me begin by saying that I never would have thought that the corruption in this country could have gotten this bad. It seems like it's everywhere! It's in our local schools, universities, in city government, state governments, national government, business, our media, the church, and the military, and the rampant corruption we are experiencing is devastating our country! I really don't think that is an overstatement. It's as if the devil has ridden into the camp under the cover of darkness and is destroying the camp from within.

Webster defines *corruption* as dishonest or illegal behavior especially by powerful people: "depravity"[22]

---

[22] Miriam-Webster, 2023

Webster defines *depravity* as: the quality or state of being corrupt, evil, or perverted.

I am going to dig deeper into the levels of corruption and depravity mentioned above, but let me first state something that I believe is very obvious: **When a nation turns from God in open rebellion, God will give that nation over to a debased mind!**

Romans 1:28–31 NKJV states it clearly:

> "Even as they did not like to retain God in their knowledge, God gave them over to a debased mind to do those things which are not fitting; being filled with all unrighteousness, sexual immorality, wickedness, covetousness, maliciousness, full of envy, murder, strife, deceit, evil-mindedness, they are whisperers, backbiters, haters of God, violent, proud, boasters, inventors of evil, disobedient to parents, undiscerning, untrustworthy, unloving, unforgiving, unmerciful".

That word *debased* in the original Greek is *Adokimos*, which means "morally worthless."[23]

So let me ask you an honest question: Does that, to some degree, describe the nation we now live in?

I heard a pastor recently say, "America is morally and spiritually bankrupt."[24] It's hard to argue against that statement.

---

[23] Strong's Concordance

[24] Dr. Jack Graham, Prestonwood Baptist Church, July 4, 2021

Let's address the corruption in America's schools. Imagine for a moment being in a time capsule for the last, say, thirty years, and just today, you have been allowed to come out and witness what is currently going on in our schools. I think we can all agree that we would be appalled at where we have come to.

In some schools we are allowing people with some of the worst morals and values in society to spend eight hours a day with our children. Frequently school boards are tyrannical groups that don't care to or want to hear what the parents think. They are pushing an agenda on the current generation that those who came before us would have never allowed, much less tolerated. Things that are now considered normal curriculum would have put someone in jail a few years ago. They are bombarding our youth with radical lies about our nation's history, their identity, their parents, God, and right and wrong, and there seems to be no accountability.

Stop and think for a few moments about the long-term consequences this will have on the current generation when they become adults and realize that they have been lied to and manipulated by teachers that they trusted and that we allowed this to happen to them!

How about our universities today? There is a very strong form of brainwashing taking place in our universities today. I have spoken to so many parents who raised their children in a conservative, faith-based environment and claim that when their kids went to college, they came back with an entirely different set of morals and values.

There is an open hostility toward conservative values, viewpoints, and ideas in our universities. America's universities have always been an environment for dialogue, debate, and the free exchange of differing viewpoints. That is no longer the case in today's American universities.

This is such a dangerous precedent! These young people will be the future leaders of the nation, and the current breeding ground of hostility, narrow-mindedness, and intolerance of different viewpoints will have a tremendous impact on the future of America.

In all levels of education, the level of corruption is staggering.

School boards have always had the very best interests of students in mind, but that's no longer the case. Driven by a radical ideology of changing America's history and a desire to control the curriculum, along with a woke agenda of silencing parents' opinions and input, these school boards are destroying what they were established to accomplish.

How about the government? This corruption has spilled over into many local city governments as well. Misuse of funds, waste, and lack of accountability have led to an environment of corruption and mistrust from the local community.

On the state level of government, we no longer can trust the outcomes of elections in many of our states. Political parties spend millions of dollars on campaigns. The level of fraud that currently exists in our state elections is staggering.

When I was growing up, we believed that local, state, and national candidates represented the very best of American values, but in today's political climate, that has become a joke. We can no longer believe the candidates or their messages. They will tell us whatever they think will get them elected, and, as in local government, there is zero accountability when they lie and break their promises.

Americans have lost confidence in the entire election process, and that is having a major impact on the country.

Jesus said in Matthew 24:12 NKJV about the very last days before His return that "Because lawlessness will abound, the love of many will grow cold." When the Bible talks about lawlessness, it can refer to man's laws, but more importantly, it refers to God's word.

Corruption is a direct form of lawlessness. And once corruption takes root in a society, it feeds off of itself and becomes rampant.

The Bible has a lot to say about corruption. It also speaks about the company we keep. In 1 Corinthians 15:33 NKJV, it says, "Do not be deceived; 'Evil company corrupts good habits.'"

When we look at the corruption on all different levels in America today, it's clear to see that those with evil intentions are corrupting good habits that have been the bedrock foundation of our nation. The effects of this lawlessness and corruption are destroying the fabric of America.

When a society loses faith in its election system and its leaders as a whole, that is a dark turning point for a nation! America is currently at this turning point.

Chapter 12

The Silent Church

—w—

This is a subject that is dear to my heart, and my heart is broken over what I am witnessing in the American church today.

As the leader of the free world for so long and as the greatest Christian nation in the history of mankind, we have always been that "beacon of light on a shining hill." Is this still the case?

As I witness the demise of America accelerating, I grieve for my nation as Jeremiah grieved for the nation of Israel during his days.

God's word is sometimes so clear and to the point that it can be a bit startling. Listen to what God says about a nation in rebellion to Him and His word.

In Jeremiah 18, the Scripture says:

"The word which came to Jeremiah from the LORD, saying: "Arise and go down to the potter's house, and there I will cause you to hear My words." Then I went down to the potter's house, and there he was, making something at the wheel. And the vessel that he made of clay was marred in the hand of the potter; so he made it again into another vessel, as it seemed good to the potter to make. Then the word of the LORD came to me saying: "O house of Israel, can I not do with you as this potter?" says the LORD. "Look, as the clay is in the potter's hand, so you are in My hand, O house of Israel! The instant I speak concerning a nation and concerning a kingdom, to pluck up, to pull down, and to destroy it, if that nation against whom I have spoken turns from its evil, I will relent of the disaster that I thought to bring upon it. And the instant I speak concerning a nation and concerning a kingdom to build and to plant it, if it does evil in My sight so that it does not obey My voice, then I will relent concerning the good with which I said I would benefit it. Now therefore, speak to the men of Judah and to the inhabitants of Jerusalem, saying, 'Thus says the LORD: "Behold, I am fashioning a disaster and devising a plan against you. Return now every one from his evil way, and make your ways and your doings good."' "And they said, 'That is hopeless! So we will walk according to our own plans, and we will everyone obey the dictates of his evil heart'" Jer. 18:1–12 NKJV.

In this section of Scripture, it is God who builds and plants or pulls down and destroys a nation. But God's actions are determined by the actions of a kingdom or a nation.

If the nation is seeking God and following His word, that nation will be blessed, and we have experienced that in abundance in America. But the flip side of that is if the nation is in rebellion to His word and committing evil then there will undoubtedly be correction and ultimately judgment, and that is what we are witnessing in America today.

In Matthew 5:13–14 NKJV, Jesus said, "You are the salt of the earth: **but if the salt loses its flavor;** how shall it be seasoned? **It is then good for nothing but to be thrown out and trampled underfoot by men. You are the light of the world**. A city that is set on a hill cannot be hidden" (emphasis added).

The church is supposed to be that salt and light that Jesus talked about, but the salt has lost its flavor, and the light has lost its brightness.

We are now living in the days of the Laodicean church! This is the lukewarm church Jesus warned about in Revelation 3:17 NKJV, "You say, 'I am rich, have become wealthy, and have need for nothing'——and do not know that you are wretched, miserable, poor, blind, and naked."

The American church today has become, to a large degree, a social club with feel-good messages about "your best life now" when alarm bells should be exploding from the pulpits that we as a nation are being destroyed from within!

If you saw your neighbor's house on fire and knew that they were asleep inside that house, would you do everything you could to get them out of there, or would you mind your own business and say nothing?

Well, I am here to tell you that the spiritual and moral house of America is in full flames, and the church of America is standing by silently and allowing it to happen! We are more concerned about not offending a group of people than we are preaching the word of God and speaking truth to a dying nation.

When is the last time you heard a message on sin, repentance, and the subject of hell and eternal fire?

The Bible says: "The fear of the Lord is the beginning of wisdom." The problem is that we have lost the fear of the Lord in the church and in our nation!

With everything that is going on right now with America, I really struggle with the question: **Where are the spiritual leaders in America today?**

The prophets in the past were treated horribly for speaking the truth, but that was their calling. They were called by God to warn the people, and they took that calling very seriously.

In chapter 2, I talked about the watchman role and how important that role is. I believe it bears repeating that if there has ever been a time in America that we need those watchmen, it is now!

I pray you can feel the urgency in my writing about this. I feel strongly that we, as a nation, are very close to being at a point of no return concerning the moral and spiritual condition we now find ourselves in.

Another reason it's critical that the church not be silent right now is regarding what Jesus said in John 3:19–20 NKJV: "And this is the condemnation, that the light has come into the world, and men loved darkness rather than light, because their deeds were evil. For everyone practicing evil hates the light and does not come to the light, lest his deeds should be exposed."

There is a darkness that has descended upon America, and it is growing exponentially day by day, week by week, month by month, and year by year. Things are happening so quickly now that it is imperative that the voices for truth must stand up and proclaim the truth from God's Word!

In conclusion, concerning the silent church, Paul spoke about the time we are currently living in when he said:

> "Preach the word! Be ready in season and out of season. Convince, rebuke, exhort, with all long-suffering and teaching. For the time will come when they will not endure sound doctrine, but according to their own desires, because they have itching ears, they will heap up for themselves teachers; and they will turn their ears away from the truth, and be turned aside to fables" (2 Tim. 4:2–4 NKJV).

That phrase *sound doctrine* means "wholesome, truthful teaching." We are now experiencing what Paul warned us about in today's world. People don't want to hear the truth from the Scriptures. Instead, they look for teachers who will tickle their ears by telling them that whatever feels right to them is ok.

Again I ask, why is the church silent about these issues at such a critical time in our nation's history?

Chapter 13

What about AI?

—◈—

I recently was asked to speak about the subject of AI (artificial intelligence) from a biblical perspective, and I was taken back by the interest and response from the listening audience, which prompted my wife Micah to suggest that I should add this chapter to my new book.

The following is straight from the speech that I gave:

* * *

"I believe we are at a very interesting point in world history right now.

There are forces that are moving in the spirit realm that will change the world society in ways that have been unimaginable in the past!

Allow me to share five reasons why I feel led to teach on this subject right now.

1. It is exploding on the scene right now.
2. Many people really do not understand what it is and the dangers it poses.

3. It will very quickly have more impact on our lives than we can imagine.
4. It is demonic!
5. Lastly, I think it is important that we look at AI from a biblical standpoint.

I have been studying this subject closely for the last few years, and I have a strong conviction about what I will share with you today.

> Daniel 12:1–4 NKJV
> Prophecy of the End Times
> "At that time Michael shall stand up, the great prince who stands watch over the sons of your people; And there shall be a time of trouble, Such as never was since there was a nation, Even to that time. And at that time your people shall be delivered, everyone who is found written in the book. And many of those who sleep in the dust of the earth shall awake, Some to everlasting life, Some to shame and everlasting contempt. Those who are wise shall shine like the brightness of the firmament, And those who turn many to righteousness like the stars forever and ever. But you, Daniel, shut up the words, and seal the book until the time of the end; many shall run to and fro, and knowledge shall increase."

Allow me to teach on this passage from the book of Daniel.

The setting here: Daniel had some very graphic, disturbing visions, and the angel Gabriel appeared to Daniel to give him some clarity and understanding of what he had seen.

The explanation is what is referred to as "future prophecy." In other words, these are about events that will take place in the future. Daniel was told that in the future, there would come a time when the world would experience trouble like it never had before.

For this teaching, I would like to focus on verse 4, where Gabriel told Daniel to "shut up the words and seal the book until the time of the end; many shall run to and fro, and knowledge shall increase." Here, Daniel was told that these words needed to be "shut up." In other words, these words do not apply right now, but they will in the future.

And then Daniel was told: "until the time of the end." This phrase "until the time of the end in the original Hebrew language denotes the very, very end of time. Then he was told why: because "many shall run to and fro" and because "knowledge will increase."

"Many shall run to and fro" refers to travel. Pause and think about something here. The first car was put into production in 1886, but before that, the main mode of transportation was walking or horseback. On horseback, the normal distance traveled might be twenty-five to thirty miles a day. So in the last 150 years, we have gone from traveling twenty-five to thirty miles in a day to thousands of miles in a day. Even fifty years ago, it was not unusual to find someone who had never been on a plane or maybe just a few times. Today, it is common for a person to have breakfast in one country and dinner halfway around the world. We travel faster, greater distances, and more frequently than ever before in history. In other words, "many shall run to and fro."

Now let us look at the phrase in verse 4 that says, "and knowledge shall increase." Once again, looking at the original Hebrew language, the word for *increase* denotes that something will increase abundantly or explode exponentially.[25]

Gabriel told Daniel that in the very, very last days, people would travel farther, faster, and more often than any time in history, and that knowledge would explode exponentially.

I, along with many other people who study the Bible seriously, believe that Gabriel was speaking about the days we are living in right now. Combine this with what Paul said concerning the end of time: "The coming of the lawless one is according to the working of Satan, with all power, signs, and lying wonders, and with all unrighteous deception among those who perish, because they did not receive the love of the truth, that they might be saved" (2 Thess. 2:9–10 NKJV). "And you He made alive, who were dead in trespasses and sins, 2 in which you once walked according to the course of this world, according to the prince of the power of the air, the spirit who now works in the sons of disobedience" (Eph. 2:1–2 NKJV).

---

[25] Strong's Concordance

I believe we are now in the midst of the "explosion of knowledge" that Daniel wrote about, and it is being done in full concert with the "lawless one according to the working of Satan, with all power, signs, and lying wonders."

Paul called Satan the "Prince of the power of the air," and AI is a tool that he will use. **It is called AI: artificial intelligence.**

Think about the concept of AI, the idea that computers can learn 24/7. While we are asleep, the computer is learning. When we are at work, on vacation, or at a ballgame, the computer is learning. Non-stop, the computer will be learning; this is the new phenomenon called AI and the path we are on with AI.

Paul warned us about the principles of the world in Colossians 2:8 NKJV: "Beware lest anyone cheat you through philosophy and empty deceit, according to the tradition of men, according to the basic principles of the world, and not according to Christ."

As believers in Christ, the Bible tells us that we should have a certain discernment. In Proverbs 2:3, we are told to "cry out for discernment" (NKJV).

The writer of Hebrews explains it this way: "But solid food belongs to those who are of full age, that is, those who by reason of use have their senses exercised to discern between good and evil" (Heb. 5:14 NKJV).

As we learn about AI, we should pray for discernment to understand exactly what the risks are and be aware of these risks.

Let's start with just the word *artificial*. Webster defines *artificial* as "Man-made" or "Imitation." [26]

I believe this is the same trick Satan has been using to deceive mankind since the garden when he said, "You can be like God." (Gen 3:5 NKJV)

Remember the Tower of Babel in Genesis 11? (Read Genesis 11:6.) It is as if God is saying: "If this is what you want to do, then go ahead. I will let you proceed down this road."

I want to read some information to you from the so-called experts on AI and the future of AI that is exploding on us as we speak! This is quite a bit of information, but I think it's important for you to read.

These statements are from a book titled *Our Final Invention* by James Barrat. [27]

* * *

Define AI

What is artificial intelligence (AI)?

Artificial intelligence is the simulation of human intelligence processed by machines, especially computer systems.

AI is a machine's ability to perform the cognitive functions we associate with human minds, such as perceiving, reasoning, learning, interacting with an environment, problem solving, and even exercising creativity. You've probably interacted with AI even if you didn't realize it—voice assistants like Siri and Alexa are founded on AI

[26] Miriam-Webster, 2023

[27] Barrat, *Out Final Invention*

technology, as are some customer service (chatbots) that pop up to help you navigate websites.

Next we have AGI:

AGI is: ARTIFICIAL GENERAL INTELLIGENCE (It is advance AI)

Agi is a machine that has the ability to understand or learn any intellectual task that a human being can, while AI is a machine that performs specific tasks well.

The following are some of the possible dangers of AI & AGI?

- Existential risk from artificial intelligence:
- Existential risk from artificial general intelligence is the hypothesis that substantial progress in artificial general intelligence (AGI) could result in human extinction or some other unrecoverable global catastrophe.[1][2][3]

The existential risk ("x-risk") school argues as follows: The human species currently dominates other species because the human brain has some distinctive capabilities that other animals lack. If AI surpasses humanity in general intelligence and becomes "superintelligent", then it could become difficult or impossible for humans to control. Just as the fate of the mountain gorilla depends on human goodwill, so might the fate of humanity depend on the actions of a future machine superintelligence.[4]

Too few people know that we need to have an ongoing international conversation about AI & AGI comparable to those we have about nuclear weapons. Too many people think the frontiers of AI are delineated by harmless search engines, smart phones, and now Watson. But AGI is much closer to nuclear weapons than to video games.

Is AGI Just Around the Corner? Experts Weigh In

Experts in the field of AI have varying opinions on how close we are to achieving AGI. Some believe that we are just a few years away. One key factor in determining the timeline for AGI is the rate of technological progress. (** Daniel 12:4 again/ my insert) If breakthroughs continue to happen at a rapid pace, we could see AGI sooner than expected.

The so-called "godfather of AI" a man named Geoffrey Hinton continues to warn about the dangers of artificial intelligence weeks after he quit his job at Google.

In a recent interview with NPR, Hinton said there was a "serious danger that we'll get things smarter than us fairly soon and that these things might develop bad motives and take control. All I want to do is just sound the alarm about the existential threat," he said.

About AGI:

Ray Kurzweil (an expert in the field of AI), believes that the shortest route to AGI is to reverse engineer the brain—intricately scanning it to yield a collection of brain-based achievements. Several organizations are working on projects to accomplish this path to AGI. He explains "There's no moral merit badge required for studying AGI."

> "They have now created AI technology that can scan your brain and know your thoughts."

THEN WE PROGRESS TO WHAT IS CALLED:
AGI SINGULARITY

AGI singularity refers to an event where the AIs in our lives either become self-aware, or reach an ability for continuous improvement so powerful that it will evolve beyond our control.

"SINGULARITY" refers to the point in time when the development of robotics and intelligent machines will become uncontrollable. In this scenario, artificial intelligence will be able to surpass the brain power of humans and will be able to evolve on its own.

On a supercomputer operating at a speed of 36.8 petaflops, or about twice the speed of a human brain, AI is improving its intelligence. It is rewriting its own program, specifically the part of its operating instructions that increases its aptitude in learning, problem solving, and decision making. At the same time, it debugs its code, finding and fixing errors, and measures its IQ against a catalogue of IQ tests. Each rewrite takes just minutes. Its intelligence grows exponentially on a steep upward curve. That is because with each iteration it's improving its intelligence by 3 percent. Each improvement also contains the improvements that came before.

During its development, the Busy Child, as the scientists have named the AI, had been connected to the Internet, and accumulated exabytes of data (one exabyte is one billion billion characters) representing mankind's knowledge in world affairs, mathematics, the arts, and sciences. Then, anticipating the intelligence explosion now underway, the AI makers disconnected the supercomputer from the Internet and other networks. It has no cable or wireless connection to any other computer or the outside world.

Soon, to the scientists' delight, the terminal displaying the AI's progress shows the artificial intelligence has surpassed the intelligence level of a human, known as AGI, or 'artificial general intelligence.' Before long, it becomes smarter by a factor of ten, then a hundred. In just two days, it is one thousand times more intelligent than any human, and still improving.

The scientists have passed a historic milestone! For the first time humankind is in the presence of an intelligence greater than its own.

It is no surprise that the Singularity is often called the Rapture of the Geeks—as a movement it has the hallmarks of an apocalyptic religion, including rituals of purification, disregarding frail human bodies, anticipating eternal life, and an uncontested charismatic leader. I wholeheartedly agree with the Singularitarian idea that AI is the most important thing we could be thinking about right now.

Dreams about eternal life throw out a powerful distortion field. Too many Singularitarians believe that the combination of technologies presently accelerating will not yield the kinds of disasters we might anticipate from any of them individually, instead they believe it will save mankind from the thing it fears most. Death.

But how can you competently evaluate tools, and whether and how their development should be regulated, when you believe the same tools will permit you to live forever? And as scholar William Grassie argues, when you are asking questions about transfiguration, a chosen few, and living forever; what are you talking about if not religion?"

"We now have the actual means of understanding the software of life and reprogramming it; we can turn genes off without any interference, we can add new genes, whole new organs with stem cell therapy," Kurzweil said. "The point is that medicine is now an information technology—it is going to double in power every year. These technologies will be a million times more powerful for the same cost in twenty years. The shortest route to AGI is to reverse engineer the brain—intricately scanning it to yield a collection of brain-based circuits. Represented in algorithms or hardware networks, these circuits will then be fired up on a computer as a unified synthetic brain and taught everything it needs to know. Several organizations are working on projects to accomplish this path to AGI as we speak."

Kurzweil claims that we'll experience 200,000 years of technological progress in a relatively few calendar years. Could we tolerate so much progress coming so fast?

He thinks it's implausible to expect that hundreds of thousands of years of evolution will turn on a dime in thirty years or less, and that we can be reprogrammed to love an existence that is so different from the lives we've evolved to fit."

The quest to create AGI is unstoppable and probably ungovernable. And because of the dynamics of doublings expressed by LOAR, (LAW OF ACCELERATED RETURNS); AGI and in turn Singularity, will take the world stage (and I mean take) much sooner than we think.

Excerpt From
Our Final Invention
James Barrat
https://books.apple.com/us/book/our-final-invention/
id647685260

* * *

Allow me to give you what I call the "good" news and the "bad" news of what I think about AI and the future. As Christians, we don't have to fear what is coming. Second Timothy 1:7 says, "God has not given us a spirit of fear, but of power and of love and of a sound mind." We are also to have the spirit of discernment that I mentioned earlier.

This is an amazing time to be alive on planet earth, especially if you are believer in Jesus Christ!

As we witness the future of technology that is exploding in our world, know this: God is in

control! He is the source of intelligence, and there is nothing artificial about our heavenly Father!"

Chapter 14
Good vs. Evil

—〰—

When we peel the onion back and truthfully examine what is happening in America today, it comes down to this: **good vs. evil!** Call it left vs. right, liberal vs. conservative, or Democrats vs. Republicans, but it really is pure good vs. evil, folks. That's why we are so divided on so many major issues. Amos 3:3 NKJV says, "Can two walk together, unless they are agreed?"

I would like to be wrong on the following statement, but I don't see either side of our divided nation saying to the other side, "Ok, you guys were right all along, and we are going to come over to your side of thinking." The issues are too great, and the opinions are too imbedded on each side. The stakes are too high for each group. The progressive side wants what they want with zero compromises, and the conservative side must stand for what God says is right and wrong, or we have walked away from our faith. This isn't politics, where each side should compromise. These are issues that are literally tearing apart the fabric of our nation.

There can't be common ground between both good and evil. There's no such thing as "Well, this is kind of good and kind of evil at the same time."

There is no such thing as a "white lie." Something is either a lie or not. There are no half-truths. It's either true or not.

Someone may say, "Craig, just because something is true for you doesn't make it true for me." I believe this statement is a deception. It's either true or not. It's either good or evil.

One of the strongest tools the devil is using right now in tearing this country apart is the spirit of deception that is engulfing our nation and world today, and I want to examine it closer. The devil uses this tool against us in a very subtle way of taking a subject and rubbing out the lines between black and white, creating what is referred to as the "gray area."

He will question you, put doubt in your mind as to whether something is true or not, and plant seeds of deception. That's what he does. That's who he is. He is a deceiver. He is a liar and is the father of lies.

When speaking to the leaders of Israel, this is how Jesus explained it in John 8:43–45 NKJV:

> "Why do you not understand My speech? Because you are not able to listen to My word. You are of your father the devil, and the desires of your father you want to do. He was a murderer from the beginning, and does not stand in the truth, because there is no truth in him. When he speaks a lie, he speaks from his own

recourses, for he is a liar and the father of it. But because I tell you the truth, you do not believe Me".

For us to defeat an enemy, we must understand some things about the enemy and how that enemy works. So, first and foremost, **we must understand and recognize that the devil is a liar!**

The devil is also very clever and cunning. He is also bold. When tempting Jesus in the wilderness, he said to Jesus twice, "If You are the Son of God."(Luke 4:3 NKJV) That is such a bold statement to make to Jesus. The devil was actually trying to get Jesus to doubt who He was!

So here is the question for us: If the devil was bold enough and audacious enough to come at Jesus and try to get Him to doubt who He was, can you only imagine what he will do to us? And if we aren't armed with the truth from God's word, how can we expect to defeat an enemy who hates us and wants to destroy us?

I mentioned that the devil is subtle. There is a saying that goes something like this: "What one generation forbids, the next generation tolerates, and the next generation celebrates." This is exactly the description of what has and is happening in America. Things that our forefathers knew were wrong became tolerated in the next generation and are now being celebrated in the current generation.

I've discussed right and wrong or evil and good in this book; let me share with you what the word says about this subject. Back in chapter 2, we looked at a verse that I want to revisit. Isaiah 5:20 NKJV says, "Woe to those who call evil good, and good evil; Who put darkness for light and, and light for darkness; who put bitter for sweet, and sweet for bitter."

It's as if the Lord is saying: "When a nation or group of people take what I say is 'good' and call it 'evil,' and when that nation or group of people take what I say is 'evil' and call it 'good,' they have pronounced their own judgment.

Please take note that it's good vs. evil; light vs. darkness. There is no gray area here. **It's good, or it's evil!**

God is a patient God. The Scripture tells us that He is "longsuffering towards us, not willing that any should perish, but that all should come to repentance" (2 Pet. 3:9 NKJV).

The choice is ours to make as a nation. America has been and still is a great nation, but we are in a free fall both morally and spiritually.

Final Thoughts
Is It Too Late?

—ɯ—

In the book of Joshua, the Lord spoke through Joshua to the nation, and toward the end of chapter 24, Joshua said to the nation: "And if it seems evil to you to you to serve the LORD, choose for yourselves this day whom you will serve" (Josh. 24:15 NKJV).

This is the question that we must ask ourselves again today as a nation. Who are we going to serve, the desires of our own hearts with no regard to what God says about right and wrong, or are we willing and able to take a very candid examination of where we are as a nation, the direction we are headed and ask ourselves this: **Is it too late?**

I make no apologies for believing in the Bible and what it says. I didn't write it; God did. In Numbers 23:19 NKJV, it says, "God is not a man, that He should lie, nor a son of man, that He should repent. Has He said, and will not He do? Or has He spoken and will He not make it good?"

Allow me to leave you with this Scripture from Isaiah. "If you are willing and obedient, you shall eat the good of the land; but if you refuse and rebel, you shall be devoured by the sword"; for the mouth of the LORD has spoken" (Isa. 1:19–20 NKJV).

The word *good* here is the Hebrew word *Tuwb,* and it means "the very best of, in the widest sense." [28]

It's as if God is saying, "It's up to you. If you are willing to obey what I say, then you will enjoy the very best of everything I have for you, but if you refuse and rebel, you will be destroyed." What God says is final. What He says will happen, will happen.

We are at a crossroads in America, and the choice is ours. Will we choose the *good* way or the *evil* way? **I pray it's not too late!**

---

[28] Strong's Concordance

Printed in the USA
CPSIA information can be obtained
at www.ICGtesting.com
JSHW011034111123
51840JS00006B/13